Teaching Primary Physical Education

5. 2012

Education at SAGE

SAGE is a leading international publisher of journals, books, and electronic media for academic, educational, and professional markets.

Our education publishing includes:

- accessible and comprehensive texts for aspiring education professionals and practitioners looking to further their careers through continuing professional development

- inspirational advice and guidance for the classroom

- authoritative state of the art reference from the leading authors in the field

Find out more at: **www.sagepub.co.uk/education**

Teaching **Primary** **Physical Education**

Julia Lawrence

Los Angeles | London | New Delhi
Singapore | Washington DC

SAGE Publications Ltd
1 Oliver's Yard
55 City Road
London EC1Y 1SP

SAGE Publications Inc.
2455 Teller Road
Thousand Oaks, California 91320

SAGE Publications India Pvt Ltd
B 1/I 1 Mohan Cooperative Industrial Area
Mathura Road
New Delhi 110 044

SAGE Publications Asia-Pacific Pte Ltd
3 Church Street
#10-04 Samsung Hub
Singapore 049483

Library of Congress Control Number: 2011933715

British Library Cataloguing in Publication data

A catalogue record for this book is available from the British Library

ISBN 978-0-85702-735-1
ISBN 978-0-85702-736-8 (pbk)

Typeset by C&M Digitals (P) Ltd, Chennai, India
Printed and bound by CPI Group (UK) Ltd, Croydon, CR0 4YY
Printed on paper from sustainable resources

For mum

CONTENTS

ABOUT THE AUTHOR

Dr Julia Lawrence has worked in initial teacher education for over ten years and is currently based at Leeds Metropolitan University. She has previously taught in Bedfordshire and Buckinghamshire.

Julia has contributed to a number of textbooks associated with supporting those training to work in the education profession, both in physical education and the wider teaching context.

Her research focuses on pupils' experiences of physical education in particular during the transition from primary to secondary school, as well as trainee teachers' experiences of initial teacher education.

FOREWORD

Teaching Primary Physical Education provides both theoretical and practical perspectives on teaching physical education in primary schools. The clear presentation and well argued positions covered in the book should help teachers in the primary school to develop their understanding of the subject and hence become reflective practitioners in relation both to their work in this curriculum area and to the contribution physical education can make to the education of primary school children. This critically reflective stance should enable them to improve their practical day-to-day teaching of the subject as well as have the confidence and understanding to take on leadership roles in physical education, arguing for its unique and significant place in the curriculum.

This is a particularly valuable text as little has been written on the philosophy underpinning physical education in the primary school. Most recent research, debate and text books about physical education centre on secondary education. There are a number of reasons for this, including the fact that physical educationists involved in secondary school are specialists who have followed an in depth study of the subject, whilst there are very few teachers in the primary school who have specialist knowledge of the subject area. Primary teachers are, in the main, generalists who have to cover the whole curriculum. These teachers have had minimal time to reflect on physical education on account of the multiple demands on their time in training and in school. Regrettably this lack of training has resulted in lack of knowledge of the movement and its importance in the all-round education of the child.

This leaves the impression that physical education in the primary school is of less importance than that in the secondary school. This is far from the truth. Physical education in the primary school is the critical foundation for work at secondary level and can establish attitudes to involvement in physical activity that can persist throughout life. There is an urgent need for scholarly work in the area of physical education in the primary school to enhance the teaching and standing of the subject. I therefore welcome this book in adding to the literature available on physical education in primary schools.

Susan Capel
Professor and Head of School of Sport
and Education, Brunel University

INTRODUCTION

The teaching of physical education in primary schools has always be debated and questioned. Proposed changes to national curricula and continuing debates around physical activity and healthy active lifestyles suggest that a rise in the importance of physical education as a core subject may be just round the corner. This book provides an overview of key aspects associated with the development and delivery of effective physical education experiences.

Chapters 1, 2 and 3 provide a theoretical perspective on physical education looking at not only a rationale for the inclusion of the subject within education, but also a review of theories of learning and development associated with the subject as well as the range of teaching approaches that can be used to create effective learning opportunities.

The diverse nature of pupils is explored in Chapter 4 where consideration is given to providing learning opportunities reflective of the needs of all pupils. This is supported by Chapter 5 which covers the health and safety aspects of delivery.

Chapter 5, 6 and 7 look at the development of specific skills through physical education building from the development of basic motor competences to the skills associated with physical education.

Chapter 8 draws together the previous chapters by looking at how the concepts and activities explored are integrated and reflected in the planning process.

Chapters 9 and 10 explore education in the contribution of physical education to the wider curriculum and cross-curricular themes, as well as links to the wider community. To conclude, Chapter 11 looks at how you might develop as a subject leader within physical education.

Throughout the book practical activities, case studies and extended readings provide you with an opportunity to reflect upon your own learning and development, while materials available from the companion website provide further support. This can be found at www.sagepub.co.uk/lawrence and by clicking on the Sample Materials tab.

 Companion website

Support materials for Chapter 2

• Examples of resource cards

Support materials for Chapter 3

• Sport Education

Support materials for Chapter 4

• Behaviour management strategies
• Keywords for areas of activities
• Differentiation strategies

Support materials for Chapter 5

• Activity specific websites
• Warming up and cooling down activities
• Entering and exiting pools
• Examples of risk assessments

Support materials for Chapter 6

• Resources for developing motor skills

Support materials for Chapter 7

• Resources for athletics
• Resources for dance

- Resources for games activities
- Resources for gymnastics
- Resources for swimming
- Resources for problem solving
- Resources for orienteering

Chapter 8

- Lesson planning templates

Chapter 9

- Promoting cross curricular themes

CHAPTER 1

WHY PHYSICAL EDUCATION?

Chapter aims

- To define physical education
- To develop an understanding of the role and benefits of physical education
- To provide opportunities for you to reflect upon your personal experiences of physical education
- To develop an understanding of changes in physical education over the last century

---

For many of us, our experiences of physical education have shaped the way we feel towards the subject. At times during your schooling, you probably questioned why you had to do the subject at all, especially when it was too cold, raining or too hot! For some of you, it was more about the relevance of the activity. Why was physical education on the curriculum? Why did you have to run the 1500m? These are questions that were asked but possibly never really answered.

If we as practitioners do not understand why we are teaching a subject, there is potential for our values to impact on the experiences of those whom we teach. It may become difficult for us to motivate not only ourselves, but also our pupils. Therefore before we start to look at the teaching of physical education within the primary school, we must define and explore the concepts associated with the subject, and understand how physical education has evolved over time. In doing so we can start to reflect upon our own perception of the subject.

The aim of this chapter is therefore to provide the opportunity for you to develop a clearer understanding of physical education as a curriculum subject. It will allow you to reflect upon your own and others' experiences of physical education. By the end of the chapter you should be able to provide a clear rationale for the inclusion of physical education within a school curriculum.

Defining physical education – its aims and benefits

In working to construct a definition of physical education it is important to review current literature in the field. It is also important to understand that physical education can, and does, mean different things to different people. Alongside physical education you may also see references made to Physical Activity (PA), Physical Literacy (PL), Physical Education and School Sport (PESS), Physical Education School Sport and Community Links (PESSCL) or Physical Education and Sport Strategy for Young People (PESSYP). Such terms may be used interchangeably in the context of the physical education environment and therefore definitions for these will be provided within this chapter.

Physical education at the turn of the 20th century focused on physical training. Curriculum content encouraged the development of motor competences through gymnastic-based and drill-style activities. Such practice was reflective of the Swedish Gymnastics movement. A lesson would typically be composed of a series of drills, for example arm rotations or trunk rotations, with activities being taught outside. It is interesting that there has been a revisiting of some aspects of such lesson structures in the development of group participation activities such as Wake Up Shake Up (www.wakeupshakeup.com). The 1970s and 1980s saw a movement towards a much more games-focused approach, a tradition that is still evident in school curricula. The 1990s onwards focused on the development and revision of the National Curriculum designed to promote commonality and consistency in provision. This will be covered in much more depth later in this chapter, but it is important to note how this change focused on allowing pupils to develop an understanding of planning, evaluation and participation in a range of areas of activities which included athletic activities, dance, games, gymnastic activities, outdoor and adventurous activities (OAA) and swimming.

Currently a more multi-skilled approach is beginning to be viewed as beneficial in which emphasis is placed on the development of the child as a whole, and developing the breadth of motor competences necessary to perform across the range of physical activities (see Chapter 6 for more details).

At the time and within the prevailing education context, all approaches were seen to offer the core aims of physical education. However, research and personal reflections have allowed individuals to review and revise the processes involved in the subject, looking again at the potential benefits of physical education and most appropriate methods of delivery. These concepts form the basis of this textbook, for example Chapter 2 focuses on the concept of learning and how this is reflected in pupils, with Chapter 3 providing an overview of the range of teaching approaches commonly used in physical education.

Perhaps the first thing to do when looking to define physical education is to reflect upon your own personal experiences. Task 1.1 will help you do this.

 Task 1.1

1 Using your own experiences to provide examples, reflect on what physical education was like for you in the following contexts:

   a primary school
   b secondary school
   c outside of school.

2 From these experiences identify the following:

   a your positive experiences
   b your negative experiences.

3 What impact did these have on your participation?
4 Think about ways in which you will modify your own teaching to reflect these experiences.

The experiences you had of physical education will vary across phases of education (between primary and secondary school), as well as between contexts (what you did in school compared with what you did outside of the school day). Some of these experiences may have been positive while others may have been negative. If you have had the opportunity to discuss these experiences, you may well have found that they differed between males and females. It is crucial to understand that our previous experiences will have shaped our values and attitudes associated with physical education, and these may well impact on the way we subsequently deliver the subject. It is therefore important that we scratch the surface and look at how physical education is defined in the context in which we work.

The Department for Education and Employment (1999) suggests that:

> Physical education develops pupils' physical competence and confidence, and their ability to use these to perform in a range of activities. It promotes physical

skilfulness, physical development and a knowledge of the body in action. Physical education provides opportunities for pupils to be creative, competitive and to face up to different challenges as individuals and in groups and teams. It promotes positive attitudes towards active and healthy lifestyles. (1999: 15)

But what does such a broad overview look like in reality? What is clear is that in terms of the governmental thinking of the time, physical education was seen as a vehicle for addressing issues such as the physicality of individuals – which included not only their skill development, but also their knowledge of their body – and that physical education could address wider issues concerning the engagement of individuals with others and their society, particularly how they worked together.

In some respects therefore DfEE (1999) was identifying physical education as being more than just participating in an activity. Such a premise is supported by Corbin who suggests 'a physically educated person must be fit, be skilled, know the benefits of physical activity, and value physical activity' (2002: 134). More recently Whitehead (2004) has argued that physical education is more than just the learning of specific sport-related skills. While successful participation in physical education may be an initial aim of the curriculum (indeed it was highlighted as a key focus in original National Curriculum documentation published in 1991), it is the development of pupils' abilities to assess their own and others' performance, take increasing responsibility for their own progress and finally apply their knowledge in increasingly challenging situations that allows them to develop what is commonly referred to as higher order thinking skills (Corbin and Lindsey, 1997). It is therefore evident that physical education has the capacity to provide learning experiences across the range of pupils' developmental domains (see Chapter 2) and that it is the ways in which physical education is delivered that will be most influential on the learning that takes place (see Chapter 3 Approaches to the Teaching of Physical Education).

A more recent review of the educational benefits of physical education (Bailey et al., 2006) argues that the strength of the subject lies in the development that pupils can experience physically, socially, affectively and cognitively. They argue that as pupils engage in a range of physically active pursuits during the school day, the overall physical education of the individual can be seen as much more than the activities they are taught or experience within the school curriculum. In fact the knowledge, skills and understanding that they develop during curriculum time can be applied in a range of differing contexts, for example during playtime, after school and away from the school environment in respect of any extra-curricular classes they may attend during the evening or at weekends. Such a premise reinforces what we have already started to highlight, namely that physical education is much more that participating in specific activities.

In this regard, some researchers (Whitehead, 2004, 2005; Haydn-Davies, 2005) have argued that rather than physically educating pupils, which suggests 'mastery of a measurable profile of achievements, of a prescribed set of skills'

Table 1.1 Key characteristics of physical education and physical literacy

Bailey et al. (2006)	Whitehead (2004)	Corbin (2002)	Haydn-Daves (2005)
Physical development	Motivation	Fitness	Attitudes
Social development	Confidence	Skills	Skills
Affective development	Competence	Values	Understanding
Cognitive development	Knowledge	Attitudes	
	Understanding		

(Whitehead, 2004: 5), a move should be made towards developing physical literacy, that is 'motivation, confidence, physical competence, knowledge and understanding to maintain physical activity throughout life' (Whitehead, 2009).

In reviewing a range of literature we can start to draw out some of the core aims and benefits of physical education. Table 1.1 attempts to do this with Task 1.2 providing an opportunity for you to reflect in more depth on your own thoughts on the aims of physical education.

 Task 1.2

1 Look at the different aims of physical education in Table1.1 and identify the similarities and differences in current thinking.
2 Identify what you feel are the key aims of physical education.
3 Think about how these aims are reflected either in your current teaching of the subject, or in your previous experiences of being taught physical education.
4 Discuss these with a colleague to come up with some common aims.

As alluded to earlier in the chapter, when looking to define physical education, it is important to explore other terms commonly associated with the subject. The next section makes an attempt to do this.

Physical education terminology

PA is associated with any activity that means that your body is working harder than normal.

> Any force exerted by skeletal muscle that results in energy expenditure above resting level. The term physical activity therefore includes the full range of human movement, from competitive sport and exercise to active hobbies, walking, cycling, or activities of daily life. Physical activity *per se* is a complex, multi-dimensional behaviour. (Department of Health, 2004: 81)

Daily recommended levels of physical activity are published. In the United Kingdom the recommended level of physical activity for a child and young people is:

> a total of at least 60 minutes of at least moderate intensity physical activity each day. At least twice a week this should include activities to improve bone health (activities that produce high physical stresses on the bones), muscle strength and flexibility. (Department for Health, 2004: 10)

Within this published report, guidance is provided on the type of activities that can be undertaken, as well as the levels of intensity for the activities. While the guidance is for an hour of physical activity per day, this can be made up of a series of smaller blocks of time, for example walking or cycling to and from school, playground activities and pre-lesson activities (such as WakeUp ShakeUp).

What is clear, however, is that physical education has the potential to influence PA levels. If we refer to Table 1.1, one of the key characteristics of the subject is the influence it can have on the attitudes pupils hold towards it. If the experiences of the subject are positive, it is likely that pupils will hold a positive attitude towards it, resulting in a willingness to persist with it. However, we also need to acknowledge that in terms of the recommended physical activity levels we are not necessarily going to be able to achieve these within our lessons. Therefore it is important that we look to develop links with other organisations to support the development of the child away from the school environment.

PESSCL, established in 2002, had the aim of raising sporting opportunities for children and young adults. It suggested the following:

> PE, and sport in schools, both within and beyond the curriculum, can improve:
>
> - pupil concentration, commitment and self-esteem; leading to higher attendance and better behaviour and attainment;
> - fitness levels; active children are less likely to be obese and more likely to pursue sporting activities as adults, thereby reducing the likelihood of coronary heart disease, diabetes and some forms of cancer; and
> - success in international competition by ensuring talented young sports people have a clear pathway to elite sport and competition whatever their circumstances. (Department for Education and Skills 2002: 1)

This strategy was superseded in 2008 by the PESSYP. The key aim of this strategy was to extend the current provision of two hours' high-quality PESS to a five-hour offer comprised of two hours of curriculum and an additional three hours of extra-curricular provision.

Review of physical education provision continues to take place, and it is important as you progress through your training and professional career that you keep abreast of new initiatives and curriculum development.

Having looked at defining some of the key terms associated with physical education, Task 1.3 provides an opportunity for you to reflect upon your own definition of the subject. If you have not already done so you may wish to complete Task 1.2 to support your thinking.

 Task 1.3

1 Literature sources provide a range of definitions for physical education and its associated terms. Using the sources included within the above section and any other you may access, identify the key aspects of physical education.
2 Develop your own working definition for physical education.
3 Share this definition with others to identify similarities and differences in your interpretation of the literature.

It is clear from the literature and your responses to Tasks 1.2 and 1.3, if you have been able to complete them, that there are similarities and differences in how the subject is interpreted. You therefore need to be clear about how you define the aims and benefits of participating in physical education. Kirk suggests that 'early learning experiences are crucial to the continuing involvement in physical activity' (2005: 2). More specifically he argues that it is the development of pupils' competence within physical education during their early schooling that may ultimately impact upon their overall engagement with the subject. Our role as physical educators therefore becomes focused on ensuring that such early experiences are positive. Chapters 2, 3 and 6 will develop these concepts further.

Emerging from the aims of physical education is a focus on developing confidence and competence among pupils. Gallahue and Ozmun (1995) argue that it is the way in which the task is presented that is important. Corbin develops this concept further suggesting that 'learning skill builds confidence, but confidence is needed to build skill' (2002: 133). It is therefore important to develop a teaching environment based on concepts of personal mastery where success is reflected in the completion of a given task rather than by comparison against others. Such a premise is supported by Whitehead who argues for a 'person-centred participation model' (2005: 7). This underlines the relationship between our aims and definition of physical education and the approaches we adopt in respect of the delivery of the subject.

We have now spent some time looking at the aims of physical education. We have also started to think about the content of our curriculum, specifically at the range of other areas where physical education can be used to support development beyond mere participation. The next section of this chapter provides a brief overview of the development of the physical education curriculum over the last century.

Curriculum development in physical education

At the start of this chapter, it was acknowledged that changes in curriculum design have occurred over time. The development and introduction of the first national curriculum in 1991 (Department of Education and Science, 1991) saw a focus on planning, evaluation and participation in physical education. Pupils within the primary school were expected to participate in the six defined areas of activity which included athletic activities, dance, games, gymnastic activities, OAA and swimming. A review published in 1995 (Department for Education, 1995) saw a reduction in the range of activities taught at Key Stage 1 to dance, games and gymnastic activities, with the expectation that pupils would experience all six at Key Stage 2. The only exception here was swimming which could be taught during either key stage. Further revisions occurred in 1999 (Department for Education and Employment, 1999) with an emphasis on the development of knowledge, skills and understanding associated with the subject, focusing specifically on the acquisition and development of skills, the selection and application of skills and the development of tactical awareness as well as the ability to compose sequences of movements. The ability to evaluate and improve performance remained, and a new focus on the development of knowledge and understanding associated with fitness and health was introduced.

Most recently the Rose review (Rose, 2009) considered the integration of physical education in to a thematic curriculum within primary schools. The aim of this curriculum was to develop:

- **successful learners** who enjoy learning, make progress and achieve

- **confident individuals** who are able to live safe, healthy and fulfilled lives

- **responsible citizens** who make a positive contribution to society. (QCDA, 2010a: 4 and b: 12)

Such an approach reflected the emerging focus on the wider contributions physical education can make to the development of pupils (we look at this concept in more depth in Chapter 9). However, a change of government in 2010 led to the recommendations of the Rose review being dropped, and the curriculum is undergoing a new review which will set out a new Programme of Study for Physical Education in September 2012. It is intended that this new curriculum will first be taught in schools from September 2013. Physical education has been named as one of the core subjects of this new curriculum, alongside English, mathematics and science.

It is clearly evident from the literature reviewed and the progressions seen in curriculum design that perspectives on the subject have changed over time and as a teacher of physical education, you will find it beneficial to reflect upon why physical education is taught within the school. Task 1.4 will help you to do this.

Task 1.4

Physical education has been defined in many different ways. Each of these definitions contains different core aims and related benefits for the subject. Using these aims and benefits of physical education, provide a rationale for the inclusion of physical education as a curriculum subject within the primary school.

 Chapter summary

The aim of this chapter has been to look at defining physical education and to review changes in its focus and content over time. It has required you to identify your own aims for the subject and the ways in which these might be reflected in your personal planning and delivery. It would therefore be appropriate at this point to spend some time on the following review questions.

1 How would you define physical education?
2 Research has identified key aims and objectives for physical education.

  a How would you prioritise these aims?
  b What would be your rationale for these differing priorities?

3 Personal experiences impact upon subsequent delivery.

  a How are you going to use your personal experiences of physical education to enhance pupil learning?

4 How do you feel physical education has evolved over time?
5 Do you feel that such changes have been positive or negative?

It is important is to recognise and appreciate how you personally define and value physical education as this will impact on your motivation and delivery of the subject.

Further reading

Bailey, R., Armour, K., Kirk, D., Jess, M., Pickup, I. and Sandford, R. (2006) *The educational benefits claimed for physical education and school sport: an academic review*. London: British Educational Research Association (BERA).
This review provides a comprehensive research focused overview of physical education and school sport and the associated educational benefits.

Green, K. and Hardman, K. (eds) (2008) *Physical education: essential issues*. London: Sage.

This text provides a clear overview of physical education focusing not only on the values associated with it, but also on the wider concepts associated with equity and inclusion.

Pickup, I., Price, L., Shaughnessy, J., Spence, J. and Trace, M. (2008) *Learning to teach primary PE.* Exeter: Learning Matters.
This easy to read text-book includes a detailed chapter on physical education and its associated benefits. It builds on the content of this chapter to clearly identify how a rationale for physical education can be developed, as well as how the arguments for the inclusion of physical education in the curriculum can be addressed.

In developing your knowledge and understanding of physical education and physical literacy you may wish to access the Physical Literacy website at www.physical-literacy.org.uk which provides access to a range of article and conference presentations published by active researchers working in the field of physical literacy.

CHAPTER 2

HOW PUPILS LEARN AND DEVELOP

Chapter aims

- To develop an understanding of the domains of learning
- To develop an understanding of theories of learning
- To be able to identify a range of learning environments and their characteristics and how these may impact upon the learner
- To develop an ability to apply learning theories within a physical education context

The previous chapter explored a rationale for the inclusion of physical education within the primary curriculum and provided you with opportunities to reflect upon your own experiences of the subject. If you have taken the opportunity to discuss these experiences with others, you may well have identified similarities and differences in such experiences. These differences may have been related to the activities you had undertaken, or the ways in which the subject was presented and delivered. Implicit within your interpretations would have been your personal learning journey and how this changed over time.

The aim of this chapter is to look at the theories and processes associated with learning and how these may impact upon the delivery of curriculum subjects. We will consider the different domains in which learning occurs and the key theories associated with these. We will then look at how environmental factors may impact on learning experiences and what learning opportunities exist within the school curriculum. Throughout links will be made to the delivery of physical education.

 Task 2.1

Thinking about your experiences of education and more specifically physical education, reflect upon the following questions.

1 How would you define learning?
2 How do you learn?
3 In what areas does learning take place?

Task 2.1 invites you to start thinking about learning as a process that can occur in different domains. For example, you have had to go through a learning process in order to gain qualifications thereby developing academically or cognitively; you have learnt how to work with other people thereby developing socially and emotionally; and you may also have learnt different skills thereby developing within the psychomotor domain. Before we start to look at the specific domains of learning, it is important to develop an understanding of what we mean by learning in the context of this chapter. Learning can be defined as 'the process whereby knowledge is created through the transformation of experience. Knowledge results from the combination of grasping and transforming experience' (Kolb, 1984: 41). Sugden and Connell argue that learning occurs when a child 'progresses from an absolute beginner to a performer of relative maturity' (1979: 131). Delignieres et al. view learning as 'a transitional process, from an initial response to more effective and/or efficient patterns' (1998: 222). Learning therefore relates to the acquisition of knowledge, the storage of such knowledge and the ability to use knowledge in different situations or contexts. Furthermore learning can be seen as progressive, which suggests that it can occur in stages. In viewing learning in this way, there is an acknowledgement of the individual differences we see among those learners with whom we work, and also that the speed of progression varies among different learners. If you look at the content of the National Curriculum, you will see that such a premise is reflected in the different aspects of knowledge, skills and understanding that pupils are expected to attain through the different key stages.

Having defined learning, it becomes important to acknowledge the role the learner plays within the learning process. Katz argues that learners can adopt two roles within any learning process: they are either active and engage in 'reasoning, the process of reflection, the development and analysis of ideas' (2003: 16), which results in the development of a deeper level of understanding, or passive whereby the learner is instructed, resulting in a lack of opportunity to construct their own ideas.

In adopting a learner-centred approach to learning, we need to develop a clear understanding of what we want learners to achieve from a task, and present the task in such a way that the learning outcomes can be achieved. This concept will be developed further in Chapter 8 which looks at the planning of learning experiences.

Having developed an understanding of learning and the different roles a learner may take, the next section of this chapter focuses on the domains in which learning occurs.

Domains of learning

Learning occurs within three domains: the cognitive (thinking) domain (Bloom et al., 1956), the affective (social) domain (Krathwohl et al., 1964) and the psychomotor (skill development) domain (Simpson, 1971). Cognitive learning is reflected in the development of knowledge and understanding. Within this domain learning is evidenced through learners' ability to move from being able to recall data during the early stages of their development, to being able to use their knowledge to evaluate and assess their level of understanding during later stages.

Within the affective domain, learning occurs around the development of attitudes and social and emotional skills. Development is reflected in learners' increasing awareness of those around them resulting in the establishment of value systems identifying what is important to them. These value systems are then reflected in the behaviours exhibited by those learners towards themselves and others.

The psychomotor domain of learning focuses on the development of skills. Learners move from being able to copy simple skills, to being able to combine skills in increasingly complex situations resulting, at the later stages of development, in them becoming proficient in performing specific skills.

It is important to acknowledge at this point that while these domains of learning provide an opportunity to categorise learning, they are not mutually exclusive, with aspects of learning occurring across domains. For example, in the early stages of cognitive and psychomotor development, learning is evidenced through an individual's ability to recall and copy. If you review the expectations of the National Curriculum at the Foundation Stage and Key

Stage, the emphasis is also placed on pupils' ability to explore, repeat, recall and copy.

Each domain is of equal importance, although the learning environment or task presentation may prioritise learning within a specific domain. Task 2.2 provides an opportunity to reflect upon your knowledge and application of domains of learning within your own teaching.

 Task 2.2

1 Using a typical teaching day, and the lessons you have taught or observed, reflect upon which domains of learning were included.
2 Try to identify specific examples of activities undertaken and how effective they were within the lesson.
3 Where possible discuss your reflections with a colleague or peer.

Having started to look at the domains in which learning occurs, the next section of this chapter focuses on the theories associated with learning.

Learning theories

If you look at your teaching experiences to date, you will have noticed that no class or lesson is the same. When planning lessons, or learning experiences, it is important as a teacher that you have an understanding of the major theories of learning. This will allow you to plan activities based on a theoretical perspective rather than by chance. (Chapter 3 looks in more detail at the range of teaching approaches that can be adopted in physical education lessons while Chapter 8 looks at planning in more depth.) As with the concepts discussed in Chapter 1, you will need to develop a rationale for why you have chosen the adopted approach.

Cognitive domains of learning

Learning theories associated with the development of knowledge can be categorised as behaviour (behaviourist), thinking (constructivist), social interaction (social learning) and experiences (experiential). For the purpose of this chapter we will focus on the behaviourist and constructivist theories.

Behaviourist theories of learning

Behaviourist theorists argue that learning occurs as a result of changes in the behaviour exhibited by the individual. Emerging from these theories is the concept of operant conditioning, whereby appropriate behaviours are rewarded, with inappropriate behaviours attracting some form of sanction. Common examples of these in a school environment are associated with behaviour management.

Supportive of the premise that learning results in some form of behaviour modification, Bandura, focused more on the role of the learner. Specifically within his social cognitive theory he argued that 'people are more likely to exhibit modelled behaviours if it results in valued outcomes than if it has unrewarding or punishing effects' (2001: 24). It is important that we acknowledge the modelling aspect of his theory through the expectations we set our learners as well as ourselves. Bandura's theory can be interpreted to suggest that 'children model their behaviour on what they see and hear around them, choosing behaviours they identify as positive in respect of desirability' (Lawrence, 2009: 71). Crucially, therefore, we must provide appropriate role modelling if we are to achieve the expectations of our pupils. Within a physical education context this might be reflected in the establishment of clear routines around the kit pupils are expected to wear, or the way pupils enter and leave the changing rooms. Equally it can be related to the ways in which teachers behave towards their pupils, for example teachers who continually arrive late with an unprepared lesson are not demonstrating attributes such as punctuality and preparation that they are likely to expect from their pupils.

Central to these approaches is the idea that if a desired behaviour is rewarded, then it is likely to be repeated. Conversely where the behaviour is not that which is expected then some form of sanction is imposed. Within our education system behaviourist theories are predominantly applied within our pastoral systems. However, they also raise important issues around how learning is perceived and valued by both the learner and ourselves as facilitators of learning.

So how would we reflect and develop behaviourist theories within our delivery of physical education? If we look first at the work of Bandura (1989) we want to be setting clear expectations around the behaviours we expect from pupils, for example the bringing of correct equipment and behaviours expected within the changing rooms. By setting and modelling such behaviours we provide benchmarks for pupils to assess their own performance. This allows us to look at the sanctions we impose when the behaviour is not demonstrated. Many schools have consequence charts where pupils are clearly shown the consequences of their behaviours. However, with any behaviour management, we must be consistent in our approach, to avoid giving out mixed messages.

Task 2.3 provides you with an opportunity to reflect in more detail on your application of behaviourist theories in practice.

Task 2.3

1 From your current experiences, identify five examples of the application of a behaviourist learning theory.
2 Think about what behaviour was modified and how, then look to identify ways in which you will apply such an approach within your own teaching.

Constructivist theories of learning

Constructivist theorists (for example, Piaget (1898–1980), Vygotsky (1896–1934) and Bruner (1915–) argue that learning is constructed, and occurs as a result of progression through a series of stages. According to Piaget, learning occurs as a result of interactions between the individual and their environment. However, Vygotsky and Bruner argue that the interactions occur between the individual and others, within a social environment. Vygotsky argues that the society and culture of the individual's environment strongly influence their learning experience. This is referred to as a social constructivist approach and is reflected throughout the theories of Vygotsky and Bruner. You may wish to take some time to look again at the National Curriculum and how these theories of learning are reflected in programmes of study.

Use Task 2.4 to think about your own experiences.

 Task 2.4

Vygotsky argues that learning reflects the social and cultural influences of the learner's environment.

1 Reflecting on your own learning, what social and cultural influences impacted on you?
2 Try to think how these might now impact on your delivery of physical education.

Piaget's theories are associated with learning occurring as a result of exploration and experimentation, and within this four key stages are evident. He argues that over time children develop from using basic aspects of sensory and reflexive learning to hearing the ability to make links between objects and contexts. This allows them to develop the ability to adopt and adapt appropriate knowledge and understanding. Garhart Mooney develops this further suggesting that 'children learn best when they are actually doing the work themselves and creating their own understanding of what's going on, instead of being given explanations by adults' (2000: 62). Therefore when planning, there is a need to provide such opportunities within the learning experience.

Chapter 8 looks at the development and planning of the learning experience in more depth.

Another key feature of Vygotsky's theory, published in 1978, is the concept of a zone of proximal development (ZPD). Garhart Mooney defines this concept as 'the distance between the most difficult task a child can do alone, and the most difficult task a child can do with help' (2000: 83). If learning is to be achieved, learners must be engaged in an activity which challenges them. Setting a task that is too easy or too difficult would result in frustration and an absence of effective learning. Again it is quite easy to think of examples when you might have experienced this. There will have been times when you have set pupils an activity which they completed very quickly, but because you have scheduled it to last a set period you did not move on to the next activity resulting in pupils becoming disruptive. In contrast you may have set an activity which you understood, but when it came to pupils actually doing the activity their performance did not reflect your expectations. While this could have been a communication issue, it may well have been that you had overcomplicated the activity. It is important to differentiate the tasks you provide in order that all learners have the opportunity to succeed. While tasks could be differentiated to support the learner, the second part of the definition of the ZPD identifies the opportunity for learning to be supported by others. Vygotsky also explores the concept of the expert in the learning experience, defining this individual as anyone with a greater level of knowledge than the learner. This individual may well be a learner in the same class, which offers the opportunity for peer teaching to occur. An example in physical education may be the use of reciprocal activities whereby pupils work in pairs providing feedback and guidance on performance and improvements that could be made (see Chapter 3 for more information on this teaching approach practical: examples of this are also included in Chapter 6).

Bruner develops these concepts further, arguing for the need to provide structured learning opportunities that build progressively. His concept of a spiralling curriculum proposes that learners should revisit concepts and processes progressively, but at increasing levels of difficulty to allow them to develop a deeper level of understanding. He suggests the concept of scaffolding, 'a flexible and child-centred supportive strategy which supports the child in learning new things' (Smith et al., 1998: 431), which requires the teacher to provide a series of structured activities that build upon the learner's existing knowledge base. This approach will be developed further in Chapter 3 and also in Chapter 8 which looks at planning. An example would be the setting of progressive practices or challenges that allow pupils to build on their level of skill without becoming too competitive, which may result in a decline in overall skill performance.

The theories discussed above place the learner at the centre of the process. The teacher acts as the facilitator of learning opportunities or experiences. Within a physical education context we need to look closely at the tasks we set, and think about how they build upon previous experiences. We need to think about the interrelatedness of the skills we ask pupils to perform, in order that they can make connections between these skills. If we look to apply this in the context of jumping, we might ask pupils to think about instances when we might jump, for example to catch a ball, to head a ball, jumping on and off a piece of equipment or when we are doing athletics. By doing this, we are asking pupils to think about their previous experiences and therefore build upon them. We can then get pupils to go away and think about how they jump, thus providing them with the opportunity to think about the specific skill and practise its application. Examples such as these will be explored in much more depth in Chapter 6.

Affective domain of learning

When looking at development within the affective domain we are focusing on aspects of emotional development. Sheridan (1991) argues that affective development is of at least equal importance as cognitive development. This is not a new concept. Piaget and Inhelder suggest: 'The affective and social development of the child follows the same general process [of cognitive development], since the affective, social, and cognitive aspects of behaviour are in fact inseparable' (1969: 114). Central to Sheridan's view is the need for pupils to 'gain positive self-concept, greater self-esteem and a more developed sense of competency' (1991: 29) and that 'these key facets of personality development are crucial to children's attitudes concerning learning and their sense of motivation for applying their skills in learning situations throughout life' (1991: 29). Katz suggests that 'experiences of the early years of life have a powerful influence on the later ones' (2003: 15). Consequently the learning experiences we provide have the potential to impact on children's lifelong learning experience. Such a premise builds on the work of Kirk (2005) and Corbin (2002) which we looked at in Chapter 1. It highlights the need for teachers to build confidence and the importance of effective early learning experiences if continuing participation is to be encouraged.

Within this domain we are looking at the development of learner's emotional aspects, specifically their attitude and feelings towards themselves and those around them. One of the key theorists associated with this is Erik Erikson (1995). Erikson identified eight stages of emotional development, aligned to conflict resolution or crisis. With reference to the primary environment, he acknowledged that changes in the affective domain were associated with learners becoming more independent, developing the ability to cope with the demands of the environment in which they learn and to interact with others, and beginning to establish their own identity (Keenan and Evans, 2009). Therefore effective learning experiences should include opportunities for the development of more pupil-centred and interactive activities (see Chapter 3 for the range of different teaching approaches).

Sheridan (1991) acknowledges a need to consider how the expectations of learners, which are reflected in the way we present tasks, can impact upon pupils' development, specifically how we provide feedback upon and acknowledge learners' achievements. This is closely linked to behaviourist theory and requires learners to reflect on their own self-efficacy, self-esteem and motivation.

Learners' willingness to engage in learning activities depends heavily upon the values they associate with the activity. You will know from your own experiences that if you enjoy something and see it as being beneficial you are more likely to persist with it, even when it becomes challenging, than when you are asked to do something that you see as irrelevant. This is sometimes referred to as the effort–benefit ratio (Fox and Biddle, 1988).

Within his social cognitive theory, Bandura (1989) developed the premise of observational learning arguing that learning is affected by the attention applied, the retention of the information, the translation of this learning into different contexts and the motivation to continue to engage within the learning. Additionally Erikson (1995) identified the use of social comparison between the self and others as an influential factor in the formation of identity.

When structuring activities around the affective domain, we need to think carefully about the activities planned and the impact that they might have. Physical education is a very visual subject. The nature of the learning experiences provided allows for a high level of social comparison, especially when we are asked to demonstrate or perform to the rest of the class. I am sure that you can remember having to perform your gymnastics sequence at school. For those of you who had a less than pleasurable experience of physical education, much of it may have been related to aspects of affective development, for example changing rooms, having to wear a certain uniform, feeling less able than others in your class. As practitioners within physical education you therefore need to be sensitive and acknowledge this domain within your teaching.

Psychomotor domains of learning

The final domain of learning occurs around psychomotor development. Here we are looking at how the learner develops specific skills. As with all aspects of development, learning is progressive. Gallahue and Ozmun (1995) argue that in the context of physical education such stages encompass the movement from reflexive to rudimentary actions, through to the development of fundamental skills and finally to specialised skills. Their work builds upon that of

Haywood (1986) who identified a transition from basic locomotion and move-ment skills during early childhood (ages 1–8) to the development of strength and improved efficiency during late childhood (ages 8–18). It is important to acknowledge that learning within this domain is not just associated with phys-ical education but is also focused on motor skills in general. Chapter 6 explores these concepts in more depth.

It is also important to acknowledge the impact learning within this domain may have on other domains, especially the affective domain. Early research (Breckenridge and Vincent, 1965) identified that demonstrations of physical competence (in the context of physical education the ability to perform skills) positively impact on the confidence of the individual. If we refer back to the previous section on affective development, we can infer that a confident indi-vidual is more likely to engage in social interactions. If we go back further to the section on cognitive development, we can argue that this increased confidence in social interactions would impact upon development in this domain as well.

Section summary

So far this chapter has provided a general overview of the theories of learning and the impact these may have within physical education. What emerges is that there are commonalities between theories and therefore adopting one specific theoretical perspective may not always be possible, or appropriate. Equally the domains of learning are interrelated and not mutually exclusive. It therefore becomes important during the planning of any learning opportunity that consid-eration is given to the impact of these on the developmental needs of the learn-ers with whom you work. Chapter 8 explores these concepts in more depth.

Learning preferences

We have established that learning is staged and that movement through these stages will depend upon the individual learner. Linked to this is the fact that learners have preferred learning approaches. If you think again about your preferred approach to learning it may well be different to those of others. Traditionally these have been seen as the visual (V) (reading/seeing), the audi-tory (A) (listening) and the kinaesthetic (K) (doing), shortened to VAK. Fleming and Mills (1992) developed the concept further arguing that the visual was better described as two, allowing reading (R) to be a discrete preference resulting in VARK.

Learning preferences allow us to think about how we present tasks to pupils. If we think about pupils who learn best through the visual medium, tasks need to be presented or supported with written text, for example in physical educa-tion resource cards may be provided to support the learning of a new skill.

Pupils will be able to see how key aspects of the skill are performed as well as being given key words or explanations of the skill (see the companion website for examples of resource cards). In reflecting the needs of the auditory learners, verbal explanations of the skill would be given. Kinaesthetic learners would need to be able to practise the skill.

In looking at learning preferences we start to acknowledge the range of teaching approaches that need to be adopted to reflect the diversity of pupils. Gardner (1999) identified that as well as learning preferences, pupils also demonstrate learning across a range of 'intelligences'. In this regard Gardner (1999) identified that intelligence could be reflected both in knowledge acquisition and in creation.

Gardner identified seven intelligences.

- Traditional intelligence:

  o Linguistic – learners demonstrate knowledge through the use of language, for example they may be asked to write about a specific skill or a match report.
  o Logical mathematical – learners demonstrate knowledge through their ability to solve problems, for example they may be asked to identify different ways of passing an opponent.

- Artistic intelligence:

  o Musical – learners demonstrate an appreciation of musical interpretation, for example they may be asked to choreograph a short dance sequence.
  o Bodily kinaesthetic – learners demonstrate knowledge through the ability to perform physical skills, for example they will be required to demonstrate their ability to perform specific skills.
  o Spatial – learners demonstrate knowledge through their understanding of the use of space, for example they may be asked to develop short gymnastic sequences using a defined set of equipment and space.

- Personal:

  o Inter-personal – learning reflects understanding of working with others, for example learners may be asked to work in groups of different sizes and with different peers.
  o Intra-personal – learning reflects an understanding of an individual's own personal development, for example they may be asked to reflect upon their own performance and offer suggestions as to how they might make improvements.

Task 2.5 asks you to think in more depth about your preferred approach to learning and also how you reflect different approaches to learning within your own planning.

Task 2.5

Reflect on the classes you have taught.

1 How has an acknowledgement of different learning styles been reflected in your planning?
2 Have you predominantly provided learning opportunities that you yourself prefer, or do they reflect the learning needs of your class as a whole?

Barriers to learning

So far we have identified the processes and preferences associated with learning. However, it is equally important to look at the barriers some pupils have to learning. While this is covered in much more detail in Chapter 4, a general overview is now provided.

The Department for Education and Skills (DfES) identifies: 'Difficulties in learning often arise from an unsuitable environment – inappropriate grouping of pupils, inflexible teaching styles, or inaccessible curriculum materials' (2004: 31). As practitioners we need to reflect on how we make learning accessible to pupils. This may require us to reflect upon the areas of need identified within the 2001 code of practice (DfES, 2001). This suggests that barriers may be associated with development within the cognitive, affective and psychomotor domains of learning. In some respects this brings us full circle. Having looked at domains of learning we can now consider how development within these may impact on the learner's ability to access learning.

Learning environments

While we as teachers tend to focus on learning occurring within the curriculum, acknowledgement needs to be made of other learning opportunities that exist (Chapter 9 explores these in greater depth). For many learners the knowledge, skills and understanding that they develop may occur outside the confines of the classroom. On average pupils are only in the school environment for six or seven hours per day. Examples where pupils may participate in physical activity outside the classroom include attending out-of-school clubs, playing for a local team or participation in physical activity encouraged by their parents. Residential activities organised by a pupil's school may also support learning across the domains.

While traditional learning environments have focused on classroom-based opportunities, and for physical education this may also include the school hall, gym, playing fields or playground, much social learning may occur outside the confines of the classroom through informal play opportunities. Take time to look at the interactions that take place before class and during break and lunchtimes. Opportunities for learning outside the school environment can also occur through educational trips and residential activities. While the planning and organisation of these raise issues around safe practice (see Chapter 5), such environments also widen the breadth of learning opportunities and learning experiences.

 Chapter summary

Smith et al. argue that 'physical education can and should contribute to the physical, emotional, social, moral and intellectual development of pupils' (1998: 169). This chapter has explored aspects associated with learning focusing not only on the theoretical premises of learning, but also on the practical application of them within a physical education context.

Key themes that emerge from the process of learning demonstrate that learning is progressive and that stages of learning and development are individual, and as such we cannot adopt a one-size-fits-all approach. Clear similarities are evident between the theories, allowing us to identify that any learning experience that focuses on one particular domain would not necessarilly preclude learning within other domains. This concept is developed in much more detail in Chapter 3.

We have looked at how learning can occur across a range of environments, and that exposure to these will impact upon the lifelong learning opportunities for those with whom we work. Much of what has been covered in this chapter will be developed within subsequent chapters, so it may be useful to reread this chapter from time to time. However, to review your learning in this chapter you may wish to respond to the following questions:

1 Using practical examples to support your response identify two key theories associated with the way pupils learn.
2 Explain in your own words the different domains of learning, and how these can be reflected in the planning and delivery of effective learning experiences.
3 Review the range of learning environments you have experienced as a pupil, during you initial teacher education or when you have been teaching. Identify the key characteristics of these environments and the specific opportunities for pupil development they allowed.

Further reading

Galton, M. (2007) *Learning and teaching in the primary classroom*. London: Sage.
This text provides an overview of learning and teaching in primary schools. It focuses on the range of teaching approaches to support pupil learning that can be adopted in school.

Garhart Mooney, C. (2000) *Theories of childhood: an introduction to Dewey, Montessori, Erikson, Piaget and Vygotsky*. Minnesota: Redleaf Press.
This text provides an overview of the main theories of childhood, written in an accessible way.

Gallahue, D.L. and Ozmun, J.C. (1995) *Understanding motor development: infants, children, adolescents, adults*, 3rd edn. Iowa: Brown and Benchmark Publishers.
This text breaks down the basic concepts of motor development. It provides examples of expected progressions of development through clear pictorial representations that can be adapted and used not only for observation of pupils and their development, but also to support pupils' assessment of their own and others' performance.

CHAPTER 3

APPROACHES TO THE TEACHING OF PHYSICAL EDUCATION

Chapter aims

- To develop an understanding of pedagogy in physical education
- To develop an understanding of different approaches to the teaching of physical education
- To develop an understanding of how different teaching approaches impact on the learning of individuals

---

The previous chapter aimed to develop your understanding of learning and the theories associated with it. It also provided an opportunity to look at different learning environments and how these could be applied to the teaching of physical education. If you have not read Chapter 2 for some time, you may find it useful to remind yourself of the key points raised within it by looking at the review questions at the end of the chapter.

This chapter aims to look in more detail at how domains of learning are reflected in the range of pedagogical approaches that can be adopted within the classroom and applied within the physical education context.

Pedagogical approaches to teaching

Many (Kirk, 2005; Penney and Waring, 2000; Simon, 1994; Shulman, 1987) have argued for the acknowledgement of a pedagogical approach to teaching. Simon (1994) identifies pedagogy as the science of teaching, where theoretical understanding is reflected in practical application, arguing that within the UK there is a tendency to shy away from such a concept, an argument supported by Penney and Waring (2000). In developing a concept of pedagogy, Shulman (1987) argues that within specific professions common characteristics and areas of knowledge are required and developed. In education he argues for the existence of a signature pedagogy with the emphasis placed on knowledge development and enhancement across seven key categories:

- content knowledge
- general pedagogical knowledge
- pedagogical content knowledge
- knowledge of learners and their characteristics
- curriculum knowledge
- knowledge of educational contexts
- knowledge of educational ends, purposes and values.

More recently Metzler (2005) has applied such categories specifically to the context of physical education:

- content knowledge – subject matter

- general pedagogical knowledge – generic teaching methods

- pedagogical content knowledge – subject specific teaching methods

- knowledge of learners and their characteristics – learning as a process

- curriculum knowledge – how content develops

- knowledge of educational contexts – how context impacts

- knowledge of educational ends, purposes and values – educational goals. (2005: 52)

When looking to develop an understanding of the approaches to teaching, and specifically to the teaching of physical education, we need to acknowledge the breadth of knowledge we must acquire in order to provide effective learning experiences. While this chapter focuses on approaches to teaching, references are made throughout to other chapters. In this way, it requires you to think about the connections between teaching approaches and the aims of physical education (Chapter 1) as well as how pupils learn and develop (Chapter 2).

Primary education has traditionally been seen as more pupil focused than secondary, which is seen as more subject focused. This suggests that when planning for primary lessons, the child is at the centre of the process rather than the subject. If you look at how the curriculum is structured across these phases of education, it is clear that differences do exist.

Chapter 2 looked at learning as a process and identified that most individuals will move through different stages of learning. This suggests that there must be some form of structure to the learning that takes place. Such a premise is supported by much of the work of the social constructivists Vygotsky and Bruner as well as the behaviourist theorist Skinner, and requires us as practitioners to reflect closely on what we are striving to achieve when planning our learning experiences (we expand upon this in Chapter 8).

Chapters 1 and 2 looked at how early learning experiences can influence lifelong opportunities. Kirk specifically argues that 'early learning experiences are crucial to the continuing involvement in physical activity' (2005: 2). The work of Morgan and Hansen (2008) identifies confidence among practitioners as key for quality learning experiences. This suggests that, when looking at approaches to teaching physical education we can run the risk of adopting approaches in which we feel confident rather than approaches that provide the best learning opportunities for pupils.

Educators should act as facilitators, providing structured help and guidance to support learning. Within this we need to understand the concept of readiness to learn. When looking at the approaches we adopt, we need to look at the different needs of the individuals with whom we are working. While this concept will be looked at in more detail in Chapters 4 and 8, it is important to acknowledge it here. This does not mean that we should be aiming to provide an individualised approach for all children, and nor are we suggesting a 'one size fits all' approach. What is most important is that individual differences are acknowledged, and that we ensure that the tasks planned are such that all pupils can achieve success.

Penney and Waring (2000) argue that much of the research around physical education and its curriculum is focused on the *content* of the curriculum rather than the ways in which it is taught. Furthermore they define pedagogy as 'a concept that simultaneously embraces and informs rationale, curriculum design, teaching and learning ... pedagogy is not only about the "how" of teaching, but also the "what" and "why"' (2000: 6). You will have already started looking at considering your own personal pedagogy through the development of your understanding around the rationale for physical education (see Chapter 1). Task 3.1 provides you with the opportunity to develop this further.

 Task 3.1

Reflect upon your personal definition of physical education and your understanding of the aims of physical education. Consider your current approach to teaching and think about how this pedagogical approach has been developed.

Penney (2003) argues for existence of two key categories of pedagogical approach in physical education. Firstly, expanded learning where the learner works in a context associated with criticism (questioning), discovery and practical application. In physical education this might involve pupils applying existing knowledge and understanding to practice skills or feedback on individual performances. Secondly, situated learning where pupils use their knowledge within different situations to further develop their understanding. For example in physical education, pupils might be asked to apply their knowledge of one activity when being introduced to a new activity.

Penney's categories of pedagogical approach are similar to the work of Mosston and Ashworth (1994) who identified two distinct clusters of teaching styles, i) reproductive styles where there is a reproduction of knowledge and skills through the use of decision-making, skill practice and feedback, and ii) productive styles, where new knowledge and skills are developed through the use of problem-solving and cognitive thought. The next section of this chapter will develop these concepts further.

Mosston and Ashworth's teaching styles

While generic models of teaching exist, Mosston and Ashworth's (1994) styles are specific to physical education. Their proposed approaches are based upon a spectrum characterised by the involvement of the teacher and the learner within the decision-making processes during the delivery of learning experiences. Their premise was built around the belief that 'teaching behaviour is a chain of decision making' (Mosston and Ashworth, 1994: 3). Emerging from this was a formalised structure of teaching styles. Each contained their own specific anatomy (which refers to the group of decisions that are made), including who the decision makers are, the style, and the developmental effects. It is appropriate at this point to explore these structures in greater depth in order to fully appreciate the integrity of the styles, and to provide examples of how these approaches can be reflected in the teaching of physical education.

When looking at the anatomy of the style, we are looking specifically at the decision making that occurs. Mosston and Ashworth (1994) suggest that such decisions are made prior to the lesson (pre-impact), and this is reflected in the planning of the lesson (see Chapter 8 for further detail on planning), during the lesson (impact) in terms of the progression and pace of the lesson, and after the lesson (post-impact) in the evaluative process assessing a lesson. Each learning style also considers the interactions between the teacher and learner which contribute to the decision-making process, and during which development is expected to occur. This is closely aligned to the concept of learning domains (as discussed in Chapter 2) which Mosston and Ashworth (1994) define as physical, social, affective and cognitive domains.

In selecting any teaching style for use in physical education Mosston and Ashworth (1994) felt the following questions should be addressed.

- What are my learning objectives/What do I want my pupils to achieve?
- What is the best method to use to achieve these objectives?
- How should I structure my teaching?
- How should I organise the learning?
- How do I motivate my pupils?
- How do I encourage social interactions and thinking?
- How will I know that I have achieved my objectives?

If we are to fully understand a range of teaching approaches and thereby reflect these in our planning, it is important to look at a general outline of each one in turn. This will allow you to reflect upon the basic principles and applications. The spectrum consists of 11 styles, five of which are categorised as reproductive (styles A–E) and six which are associated with the productive categories (F–K).

Reproductive styles

Style A – command
Style A, referred to as the command style, is the most direct style. Here we see the decisions being made by the teacher with an emphasis on the development of specific skills within a clear time frame. It is commonly used when there is a lot of information to be transferred over a short period of time, or when the skills being developed have health and safety issues associated with them, for example when teaching throwing skills in athletics, or a specific skill in gymnastics. In utilising such a style, self-exploration and creativity can be limited. This style is also seen as a way of managing pupil behaviour. This means that at times it is used to support less confident practitioners.

Style B – practice
Style B, or the practice style, relinquishes some of the decision making to learners as they take increasing responsibility for their own learning. As implied by its name, the style enables learners to practise a skill which allows the teacher to circulate and provide feedback to the pupils. A good example of this in physical education would be when pupils are developing their competences in throwing and catching. Once the task has been set, pupils practise the skill in pairs, while the teacher provides individualised feedback to each pair or generic feedback to the group where appropriate. While the teacher still maintains responsibility for the planning of the activity and as such the practices being undertaken, the learner has greater responsibility for the application of the skill within the practice situation. This style is used extensively within physical education teaching, and you are probably very familiar

from your own experiences of this approach; however, Task 3.2 allows you to think about this is more depth.

Style C – reciprocal

Style C, or the reciprocal style, encourages learners to work together to develop their own knowledge and understanding. As with the previous style the decision-making processes are becoming more learner focused as pupils become actively involved in the giving and receiving of feedback from their peers. As much of the feedback learners receive is from their peers, this frees up teaching time that can be used to interact and support learners. It is important that the teacher provides formalised feedback mechanisms for learners, more specifically in the form of a skill checklist (see the companion website for further details). This requires the teacher to provide a clear breakdown of the skill and its associated faults so that learners can provide detailed and specific feedback when observing. Such an approach not only engages pupils actively within their own learning, but also provides clear and sustained opportunities for them to develop their literacy skills, specifically related to speaking and listening. For example, with pupils working in pairs, one acts as the doer and performs the skill of striking a ball against a target (hitting a ball against a wall) while the other acts as an observer giving feedback based on the skill checklist provided, which might include reference to body position, arm action and leg action (see Chapters 5 and 6 for more details on specific skills). The doer then uses this feedback to make modifications to their performance, before the two swap roles.

Style D – self-check

Style D, or self-check, gives further responsibility to learners. Here, instead of receiving from their peers, they take responsibility for checking their own work. Again the teacher must make structures to support the feedback process available, but learners now have responsibility for identifying their own strengths and weaknesses and start to make decisions about progressing to the next skill. With the development of handheld video cameras within the school environment this approach allows pupils to record their own performance and then provide their own specific feedback. With this approach the emphasis is on the learner giving feedback. If we use the same example of striking a ball against a wall, the doer would now observe their performance as recorded by the observer, and using the same checklist, identify what they feel they need to do to improve their performance.

Style E – inclusion

The final reproductive style is the inclusion style, style E. Here learners are given the opportunity to select their own task and then provide personal feedback based on their completion of the task. For example, in playing a game, pupils might identify a skill which they feel they need to improve. Using checklists or other resources available to them, they can go away and practise the skill, provide themselves with feedback and then demonstrate the improvements they have made. Thus learning experiences become individualised.

Productive styles

Style F – guided discovery
Moving on to the productive styles, we start with the guided discovery style, or style F. The aim of this style is to provide learners with a series of questions which they answer to achieve completion of the overall task. In essence the style allows learners to move through a series of progressive steps to achieve a final goal. If you think back to the theories and concepts of learning, this approach links to Bruner's thoughts on learning and the use of scaffolding to elicit learning. In simplistic terms it allows pupils to discover their preferred way of performing a skill. An example here would be to ask pupils to think about the best way to hold a hockey stick. You can then provide them with a series of decisions or questions, for example 'try with both hands at the top', 'what about both hands towards the bottom?', 'is it easier to have your hands together or apart?' In responding to these questions learners will discover their preferred way of holding the stick.

Style G – convergent
Style G, the convergent style, requires learners to engage in a process of reasoning, in effect attempting to solve a problem through trial and error. Thus the style encourages the development of reasoning, critical thinking and logical thought processing. For example, pupils may be asked to think of the different ways of crossing a hazard as a means of developing problem-solving skills during OAA. Through trial and error they can identify an appropriate solution before demonstrating this to the teacher.

Style H – divergent
The divergent style, style H, engages learners in identifying multiple responses to single questions. Again the focus is on the processes of reasoning, critical thinking and logical thought, but the emphasis is on learners directing the decisions rather than being supported by the teacher. For example, pupils might be set the challenge of finding different ways of beating an opponent in a 3 v 1 situation, in which they have to work as a group to practise the different approaches before demonstrating and applying this in a more formalised game structure.

Style I – individual programme
Style I, the individual programme, engages the learner in the development of a personal programme. Examples in physical education would be the development of individual training programmes, or warm-up activities.

Style J – learner-initiated and Style K – self-teach

Finally, the learner-initiated style (Style J) develops style I further, but with a greater emphasis on learners evaluating their programme while Style K is exhibited by learners teaching themselves.

 Task 3.2

You have now been provided with a general overview of Mosston and Ashworth's (1994) spectrum of teaching.

1 Using the information contained in this chapter and the companion website material for Chapter 2, reflect upon your understanding of each approach.
2 Identify a series of activities that could be used to support each style.
3 Within your future planning try to make specific reference to styles.

Instructional models

More recently Metzler has developed the concept of instructional models. He defines these as 'designed to be used for an entire unit of instruction and includes all of the planning, design, implementation and assessment functions for that unit' (2005: 13). Within his approach he argues that learning within a model can occur across the three domains of learning – cognitive, affective and psychomotor – and that learning within these domains is prioritised dependent upon the model being used. For example, if a model encourages the use of problem solving then the cognitive domain will take priority; likewise where the emphasis is placed on group work, the affective domain will be prioritised.

Metzler (2005) suggests that this traditional or direct approach is based on the behaviourist theories. Skills are developed as a result of practice, with progression reflected in the mastery of specific skills. The teacher will model expected behaviours (skills) and feedback will be based on children's ability to perform and will focus on specific teaching and learning points associated with the given skill correcting where necessary. An example would be the teaching of a skill such as an overarm throw. As the teacher you will provide a demonstration of the skill. You will identify the key teaching and learning points:

- stand sideways
- ball held in finger tips
- opposite hand points at target
- throwing arm extends back
- rotation is from the shoulder not the elbow
- throwing arm follows through towards the intended target.

A series of practices will then be set up, for example after a defined number of successful throws you could increase the distance between paired pupils. As the teacher, you will patrol the practice giving specific feedback based on the teaching and learning points above. Such an approach is built upon the teacher as holder of knowledge and provider of opportunities for this knowledge to be developed in the learner. Learning occurs when changes in behaviours are seen. This approach clearly demonstrates aspects of Mosston and Ashworth's reproductive styles (A – E).

In his book *Instructional Models for Physical Education*, Michael W. Metzler (2005) argues that when looking at the planning and delivery of learning episodes, in this case lessons, consideration needs to be given to where the learning is taking place (context), the learners themselves, knowledge and application of theories, the domains in which learning is being encouraged, and the overall climate or environment required for learning to be achieved.

The traditional pedagogical approach to learning prioritises skill acquisition (psychomotor) and application of this skill in different situations (cognitive). What is less evident is how such an approach develops learning within the affective domain. If we think back to our own experiences of physical education lessons, time would be spent demonstrating skills and/or performing in front of other people. As a result social comparisons occurred whereby we would compare our performances against those of others. The common practice of using the best performer to demonstrate practices is an example. When using such an approach, it therefore becomes important to think carefully about who demonstrates skills, how feedback is given, for example by whom and using what criteria, and how success is demonstrated. This will significantly affect the learning climate created within the lesson, a concept explored in more depth in Chapter 8.

Teaching games for understanding

Another approach is that of Teaching Games for Understanding (TGFU) which is sometimes referred to as tactical games or 'games sense'. The concept of TGFU emerged from the work of Bunker and Thorpe (1982). The approach looks at the development of decision-making processes by requiring participants to solve a series of tactical problems through the playing of games. It is based on the premise that if the pupils are active in the learning process then they are more likely to achieve. Brunton (2003) argues that we need to provide appropriate learning opportunities that allow pupils to take responsibility for their own learning. As the teacher you therefore act as the facilitator creating the problems that need to be solved. For example, you might set the problem of exploring how many different ways there are of beating a defender in a 3 v 1 situation. Pupils can then go away and practise this to identify the most effective ways and to come up with reasons to explain their choices. They might consider the type of passes used or the position of the players. They could then apply these strategies within a game situation to gauge their level of success.

Such an approach offers pupils opportunities to demonstrate a deeper level of understanding. They can develop a greater appreciation of how they play rather than necessarily focusing on specific skill development. Thus the approach encourages self-reflection and the analysis of problems.

The TGFU model is comprised of six key steps (Griffin and Butler, 2005; Metzler, 2005):

- Step 1: Game – pupils need to be able to play games. These may be modified to reflect pupils' stages of development (see Chapter 4 for examples of how activities can be differentiated), but they need to have an understanding of what the game is and how it is played.
- Step 2: Game appreciation – contextually pupils are required to understand the components of the game. They learn to understand rules and regulations associated with the activity and adhere to these while playing.
- Step 3: Tactical awareness – pupils start to be presented with the tactical problems of the game. Pupils are required to think practically about how they would solve game specific problems. For example, they could explore different ways of passing the ball over different distances and be encouraged to think about where the best place to send the ball may be.
- Step 4: Decision making – Pupils demonstrate practically how they would solve the problem. For example, they could perform a range of different passes dependent upon the distance they need to send the ball. The focus is therefore on demonstrating what they need to do and how they will do it.
- Step 5: Skill execution – at this point pupils start to develop skills appropriate to the activity they are undertaking. Thus pupils are now able to link tactical awareness and decision making ('what' and 'how') to being able to perform the specific skills required to execute the decision.
- Step 6: Performance – pupils demonstrate their overall performance in small and large games situations.

Sport education

Sport Education, as an approach to teaching physical education, has been developed through the work of the American academic Daryl Siedentop. It aims 'to educate students to be players in the fullest sense, and to help them develop as competent, literate and enthusiastic sportspeople' (1994: 4).

Sport Education is based on the premise that individuals should experience a range of roles and responsibilities within sport. It can therefore be seen as reflecting a situational learning focus, where learning occurs as a result of interacting with different situations. The approach provides pupils with the opportunity to develop competences across a range of roles and responsibilities. The benefits of using a Sport Education approach are seen as increased investment from pupils, increased skill development and increased opportunities for marginalised pupils to become more actively involved. Interactions between staff and pupils increase with a movement away from the teacher managing tasks, allowing the teacher to increase the level of pupil–teacher interactions. Thus the teacher becomes more active in the provision of feedback. Again strong links can be made to the styles discussed earlier. However, more recently research has raised questions about the impact of the approach in respect of skill acquisition.

Practically the model involves allocating specific roles and responsibilities to pupils within a team structure. Such roles may include coach, trainer, equipment officer and team manager. Associated with each role would be a job description, for example the coach would be responsible for the development of a training programme to teach specific skills, while the equipment officer would be responsible for the organisation and collection of equipment. The lesson may be structured around practice opportunities, before the teams engage in some form of competitive situation. This competition is cumulative, resulting in the development of a league-type structure. The model is run over an extended period of time, defined as a 'season', with a culminating event occurring at the end of the season. If the model is being used across class groups, the opportunity for a festival event occurs when all teams compete together. Throughout the process the pupils actively engage in record keeping, either by developing match reports or training programmes, which encourages the development of literacy skills. Further details using an example of this model in practice can be found on the companion website.

Personalised system of instruction

A further model identified by Metzler (2005) is that of the personalised system of instruction. Such an approach allows pupils to guide their own learning and is therefore more appropriate for pupils with a developing level of cognitive ability, for example these in the older primary age range. The basis of the model is that pupils are provided with a detailed work booklet assigning them specific tasks. Throughout the process pupils are required to check their progress either through the completion of individual tasks, or tasks which require feedback from their peers or from you as the facilitator.

An example of this would be the development of a progression workbook which provides structured steps for pupils to follow as well as the use of self-check lists. This reflects similar approaches used in teaching reading whereby pupils track their own progress.

 Chapter summary

This chapter has reviewed a range of teaching strategies and models currently used in the delivery of physical education. The range of approaches is possibly more extensive than those you will have experienced as part of your own education. It is important that any teaching approach you adopt reflects the aims and objectives you have set for your class. Thus in selecting a teaching approach you need to reflect upon your individual aims and objectives, and in doing so you may find that you adopt a range of approaches within a lesson. Tasks 3.4 and 3.5 provide you with an opportunity to reflect upon teaching approaches.

 Task 3.3

The article below identifies issues that may be faced when learning to implement an instructional model. Read this article and then reflect upon your experiences of implementing a chosen model during a school experience. Some of you may be interested in exploring this as a research project at either undergraduate or postgraduate level.

McCaughtry, N., Sofo, S., Rovegno, I. and Curtner-Smith, M. (2004) 'Learning to teach sport education: misunderstandings, pedagogical difficulties, and resistance' *European Physical Education Review*, 10 (2): 135–55.

 Task 3.4

1 Having explored a number of approaches to the teaching of physical education, provide a rationale for your chosen approach.
2 Produce a medium-term plan showing how you might implement this approach within your own teaching (Chapter 8 gives you further guidance on planning).

What is clearly evident from all the approaches introduced is that as a teacher of physical education you need to have a clear understanding of the following.

- 'What do I want my pupils to learn?'
- 'Why is this important?'
- 'How and where is learning taking place?'
- 'How will I know that learning has occurred?'

In essence we are looking at the what, why, how and where of teaching. However, this chapter has only been able to scrape the surface of each model. Further readings are therefore provided below.

To summarise your learning in this chapter you may benefit from reflecting on the following review questions.

1   What are the major models of instruction used in physical education?
2   What approaches to physical education have you adopted, or observed being used on a school-based placement?

  a   What was the rationale for using this approach?
  b   What did you see as the advantages and disadvantage of the approach?
  c   How would you modify the approach in the future?

3   How would you define pedagogy?

Further reading

Griffin, L.L. and Butler, J.I. (eds) (2005) *Teaching games for understanding: theory, research and practice*. Champaign, IL: Human Kinetics.
This text provides an overview of current thinking on TGFU. Drawing on individual experiences, it provides practical examples of how the approach can be delivered.

Metzler, M.W. (2005) *Instructional models for physical education*, 2nd edn. Arizona: Holcomb Hathaway Publishers.
This text provides an overview of a range of instructional models that can be used within the physical education classroom. Providing a clear rationale for the concept of models-based instruction, it provides guidance for the implementation of the models in practice.

Mitchell, S.A., Oslin, J.L. and Griffin, L.L. (2006) *Teaching sport concepts and skills. A tactical games approach*, 2nd edn. Leeds: Human Kinetics.
This text provides an overview of the model as well as lesson plans for both games activities and levels of development.

Mosston, M. and Ashworth, S. (1994) *Teaching physical education*, 4th edn. New York: Macmillan College Publishing Company.

This text provides a clear overview of the 11 styles contained within their spectrum of teaching. It provides a range of practical application examples.

Siedentop, D., Hastie, P.A. and van der Mars, H. (2004) *Complete guide to sport education*. Leeds: Human Kinetics.

This text provides details of how to successfully implement Sport Education into the curriculum. As well as providing practical applications, it also covers planning and organisation.

CHAPTER 4

INCLUSION IN PHYSICAL EDUCATION

Chapter aims

- To develop an understanding of inclusion as a principle in physical education
- To review the range of educational needs evident in schools
- To develop an understanding of how physical education can be modified to include all pupils
- To understand the principles of differentiation

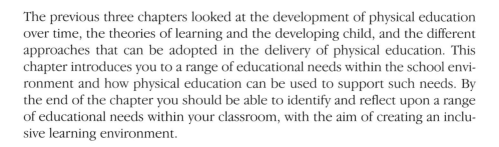

The previous three chapters looked at the development of physical education over time, the theories of learning and the developing child, and the different approaches that can be adopted in the delivery of physical education. This chapter introduces you to a range of educational needs within the school environment and how physical education can be used to support such needs. By the end of the chapter you should be able to identify and reflect upon a range of educational needs within your classroom, with the aim of creating an inclusive learning environment.

Task 4.1

1 Thinking about your experiences of teaching to date, reflect upon your current understanding of inclusion within the classroom.
2 During visits to schools, observe class teachers and identify some of the strategies they use to ensure that pupils are fully included within the lesson.
3 Use your portfolio to record your observations. As you read the remainder of this chapter, make reference to these observations to support your developing knowledge base.

Effective inclusion

The National Inclusion Framework (OfSTED, 2003: 92), identifies that effective inclusion occurs when there is:

- a climate of acceptance of all pupils
- careful preparation of placements for special educational needs (SEN) pupils
- availability of sufficient suitable teaching and personal support
- widespread awareness among staff of the particular needs of SEN pupils and an understanding of the practical ways of meeting these needs in the classroom
- sensitive allocation to teaching groups and careful curriculum modification, timetables and social arrangements
- availability of appropriate materials and teaching aids and adapted accommodation
- an active approach to personal and social development (PSD), as well as to learning
- well-defined and consistently applied approaches to managing difficult behaviour
- assessment, recording and reporting procedures which can embrace and express adequately the progress of pupils with more complex SEN who make only small gains in learning and PSD
- fully involvement of parents/carers in decision making, keeping them well informed about their child's progress and giving them as much practical support as possible
- development of and participation in training opportunities, including links with special schools and other schools.

Inclusion can also be facilitated as a result of the teacher designing suitable learning objectives (see Chapter 8), making learning accessible for all pupils and responding to the diversity of need (explored in more detail within this chapter).

A good starting point is to look at the range of educational needs evident within the classroom environment and how barriers to learning associated with such needs can be overcome within physical education.

Key groups of need within education

It is suggested that 'a child has special educational needs if he or she has a learning difficulty which calls for special provision to be made for him or her' (DCSF, 2008: 12). The SEN code of practice (2001) identifies four key groups of need within education:

- Autistic Spectrum Disorder (ASD)
- Behavioural, emotional and social development (BESD)
- Speech, Language and Communication Difficulties (SLCD)
- Moderate Learning Difficulties (MLD).

The next part of the chapter discusses these groupings in more detail, provides you with the opportunity to reflect upon your current practice and supports your professional development. It will also provide practical examples of how physical education can be modified to allow access for all pupils.

Autistic Spectrum Disorder

ASD is generally thought to be associated with developmental problems which are exhibited during both childhood and adulthood. According to the Social Policy report published in the United States of America, autistic disorder can be defined as 'the presence of deficits or unusual behaviours within three domains: reciprocal social interaction, communication, and restricted, repetitive interests and behaviours' (2010: 4). Within these three areas common behaviours may be evidenced as follows.

- Social interactions – evident through the way the individual relates emotionally to others. This may include their limited ability to communicate non-verbally and to establish peer relationships.
- Language and communication skills – reflected in the ways in which the individual may talk to others. This may include a lack of speech in general, or the adoption of alternative methods of communication.
- Physical behaviour – reflected in patterns of behaviour and routines, that if disrupted may cause distress. Such behaviours may include repetitive movements or compulsive behaviours.

It is important that you understand these behaviours if you are to engage pupils as fully as possible in your lessons. As you teach your class or classes, you will become aware of the range of behaviours evident within the pupils you teach. However, Task 4.2 provides you with an opportunity to start to collate evidence and strategies.

 Task 4.2

This chapter has given a very brief overview of the characteristics of ASD.

1 Spend some time working with the Special Educational Needs Co-ordinator (SENCO) within your school and discuss the common characteristics you would experience within the primary school.
2 Identify three key targets for development that can be included in any personal development plan you may have.
3 Make a list of common behaviours and appropriate strategies that can be employed and include these in your portfolio.

Classroom strategies

Having spent some time talking through the key characteristics of ASD we will now look at some of the classroom strategies that can be used.

Only give one instruction at a time When introducing a new skill in physical education pupils need to be given the key teaching points over a period of time, rather than all at the same time. Giving only limited information reduces the chances of information overload, and as a result limits the opportunities for the pupil to become frustrated, leading to off-task activity. Furthermore, if the pupil is asked to repeat the instructions back to you, you can assess their level of understanding. In physical education this may occur when you are introducing a practice. You may ask pupils to repeat key aspects of the practice to ensure that they understand what you have said. You will need to consider how you ask such questions and how you deal with unexpected responses but such a strategy will help you gauge the level of understanding of all pupils.

Give extra time for processing information We can often assume that pupils will process the information we give to them within a set time. However, the discussion of growth and development in Chapter 2 established that different pupils develop at different rates and therefore their ability to receive, process, retain and retrieve information will vary. Giving pupils time to think about their answers allows these processes to be enhanced. For example, when giving instructions, provide sufficient time for the pupil to take them on board and then respond. This is particularly important when asking questions. One practical application may be to introduce learning objectives (see in Chapter 8) at the start of the lesson and include the key questions you will ask the pupils at the end. This allows pupils time to think about the answer during the course of the lesson, and if you continually refer back to the question during the lesson, it will allow them time to formulate their response. You might even target specific pupils with specific questions so that they know what they are going to be asked to respond to.

Pair pupils   Another technique appropriate here would be to pair pupils so that they spend time during the lesson discussing their answers so that they have more confidence in being able to respond. For example, at the start of the lesson you might get pupils to warm up with a partner and as they are warming up to talk about the changes occurring to their body. At the end of the warm up they could be asked to identify three changes that they have experienced. By working with a partner they can gain confidence in their responses as well as being able to share their ideas.

Use established routines   All pupils need some form of structure if they are to perform effectively. Pupils with ASD struggle with changes in routines; you should therefore endeavour to establish routines and maintain them at an early stage. Examples within physical education may include when and where the pupil changes – do they go to a separate area to change and then come to the lesson with a member of support staff? Who do they work with? Do they stay with the same partner throughout the lesson?

All these strategies require careful consideration and planning, and should be used to support inclusion rather than isolate pupils. Chapter 8 looks at how we can integrate such considerations into our planning.

Behavioural, emotional and social development

Pupils who experience difficulties with BESD are defined as those who 'demonstrate features of emotional and behavioural difficulties such as: being withdrawn or isolated, disruptive and disturbing; being hyperactive and lacking concentration; having immature social skills; or presenting challenging behaviours arising from other complex special needs' (DCFS, 2008: 12). If you refer back to Chapter 2, which looked at the processes associated with development within the affective domain, you can start to make connections between what you see in the classroom and the associated stage of development.

According to DCFS (2008) common difficulties include:

- emotional disorders – depression, eating disorders
- conduct disorders – oppositional defiance disorder (ODD)
- hyperkinetic disorders – attention deficit disorder (ADD); hyperactivity disorder (ADHD)
- syndromes – Tourette's.

Classroom strategies

As with autism, a range of classroom strategies can be employed to support pupils within the school environment. Such strategies include setting clear expectations around behaviour and grouping of pupils. These will now be explored in greater depth. Supporting journals and websites are included at the end of this chapter where you will be able to access further practical support.

Set clear expectations of behaviour and reinforce these when appropriate Pupils need to be clear about their expected behaviours. Expectations need to be clear, reinforced and established as soon as possible in order to effectively manage behaviour (Chapter 5 looks at behaviour management strategies in more detail and support materials are available on the companion website). Where a pupil is seen to exhibit good behaviour this should be highlighted. This will ensure that pupils receive positive feedback and reinforcement, which may enhance the likelihood of the behaviour being repeated (you may wish to look back at Chapter 2 and the behaviourist theories of learning).

Consider pupil groupings You will need to give consideration to how you group your pupils. For example, do you want them to work in friendship or ability groups? Are there pupils who can, and others who cannot, work together? Can you give pupils different levels of responsibility within your groups (you might wish to look again at the range of teaching approaches introduced in Chapter 3)?

You will also need to consider how you get pupils into the group sizes you desire. For example, during the warm up you may do an activity that requires pupils to get into the corresponding group size to the number you call out (grouping will be covered in more detail later in this chapter). It is important that the time taken to group pupils is kept to a minimum in order that opportunities for pupils to move off task are reduced.

Task 4.3

Looking at the strategies identified for working with pupils with BESD what common approaches can you establish with the strategies used to support pupils within the autistic spectrum?

When comparing strategies you should begin to notice similar approaches that can be used to support any pupil within the classroom regardless of their defined special need. In fact it could be argued that many of the strategies identified can be employed to ensure the inclusion of all pupils within the school environment.

Speech, Language and Communication difficulties

We will now look at pupils with (SLCD).

> The ability to communicate is an essential life skill for all children and young people in the twenty-first century. It is at the core of all social interaction. With effective communication skills, children can engage and thrive. Without them, children will struggle to learn, achieve, make friends and interact with the world around them. (Bercow, 2008: 16)

Common difficulties can be associated with:

- listening to and understanding instructions and information
- learning and understanding concepts and words
- responding to questions and sharing ideas
- collaborative and social interactions.

When working with pupils who demonstrate language difficulties, we are also looking at pupils who may have English as an Additional Language (EAL). Appropriate strategies revolve around the clarity and speed of instruction. For example, when teaching pupils with language difficulties, you will need to think about the amount of information you can give at any one time. You need to consider the language you use and equally the words you would expect pupils to use in their responses. Consideration also needs to be given to the amount of time pupils are given to respond to questions. Many of the strategies used with ASD sufferers are therefore equally applicable here.

An example in physical education would be to use key words during the lesson which can be placed on walls within the learning environment to reflect the word walls that pupils would find within their main classrooms. Pupils can then be encouraged to use these words in the responses they give during the lesson. For example, in delivering a session looking at gymnastics, key words such as flight, balance, shape, jump may be displayed around the teaching space to focus pupils on the words they should use in their responses. A list of key words for different activities can be found on the companion website.

Pupils can also be encouraged to communicate through other mediums, for example through the sequences they compile in dance and gymnastics. They might be asked to produce a storyboard for their sequence where they either draw or use pre-prepared cards to show what movement they are making at each stage of their routine. This will provide not only a record of their sequence, thereby enhancing recall, but also some form of assessment opportunity.

Moderate Learning Difficulties

Pupils with MLD are identifiable by their lower than expected level of attainment in relation to National Curriculum expectations. Here appropriate strategies may include the breakdown of instructions into bite-size chunks in order that pupils are more readily able to access the information, or differentiated activities, which we look at in more detail later in this chapter. Again many of the strategies previously identified are equally applicable here.

? **Task 4.4**

1 Referring back to the tasks you have previously completed, review your understanding of SEN within the school environment.
2 Clearly identify the range of strategies that can be used to support learning.
3 Amend your action plan to demonstrate the learning that you have engaged in and the areas you feel you need to develop further.

Pupils with physical disabilities

As well as specific learning difficulties, some pupils you teach may also exhibit physical disabilities, for example visual impairments, hearing impairments or a physical impairment. Here an understanding of the level of impairment and its impact on participation is vital to ensure an effective learning experience. Each of these impairments will carry different requirements. A pupil with a visual impairment may need larger equipment to perform a task. The way we give instructions will need to be different for a hearing impaired pupil, for example you need to know their preferred communication style (which might be lip reading). Those pupils with a physical impairment may have to be provided with an adapted activity, for example the equipment may need to adapted or the rules of the game modified to provide them with a defined space in which only they are allowed to work. TDA (2009) provides a comprehensive overview of working with pupils with SEN and disabilities.

Gifted and talented pupils

Thus far we have looked at supporting pupils with educational needs that may limit their involvement. However, we also need to acknowledge that there will be pupils were work beyond the expected level of attainment. Such pupils are commonly referred to as gifted and talented. Strategies associated with accelerated learning (Smith, 1998) should be used with these pupils, for example problem solving, reflective activities, application of knowledge across differing contexts and the development of independent thinking skills. If we look back to the range of teaching and learning approaches discussed in Chapter 3, we are reminded of the principle that opportunities for learning are reflected in the approaches we adopt and that these should meet the needs of the pupils we work with.

Differentiation

The next section of this chapter looks at a range of strategies that can be employed to identify and support pupils through the process of differentiation.
  Vickerman (2010) argues that as a teacher you are:

> required to work flexibly and creatively to design environments that are conducive to learning for all. This involves identifying potential barriers to learning, teaching and assessment, whilst using strategies that offer access and entitlement to PE. (2010: 168).

Thus when looking at differentiation we need to consider: the teaching approaches adopted (see Chapter 3); the activities we are undertaking and how these might need to be adapted to reflect the range of needs; how we evaluate the learning that has taken place. Central to the process is the premise that 'all' pupils make progress, and thus we are looking at extending the performances of those identified as gifted and talented, as well as those who may be identified as working below curriculum expectations.
  While much work has been undertaken that looks at the process of differentiation Bailey (2006) gives one of the main summaries of approaches that

can be adopted. Specifically, he identifies three key differentiation groupings: organisation; presentation; content.

Organisation

A key aspect of organisation is the structuring of the learning episode in which consideration needs to be given to how you group pupils. As mentioned earlier in the chapter, this is particularly important to pupils who may have associated needs. As well as deciding how you intend to group pupils, you will also need to consider how they get into these groups. Singling out team captains and getting them to pick individuals to join their group is not the best way of either getting efficient and effective groups or enhancing pupils' self-esteem, especially if they are the last chosen. A more effective way may be to call out numbers during a warm-up activity and get pupils to make that group size. When grouping you also need to consider the activity being undertaken. For example, when practising a new skill, pupils may find it more beneficial to be working on their own in order to get the opportunity to practise the skill more frequently. If you want to put the skill into a game situation, you may wish to work with small-sided games so pupils have more opportunity to practise the skill as they will be more likely to receive the ball due to the smaller number of team mates.

A second organisational aspect is to think about the size of the area you might wish to use. When teaching physical education, never feel that everyone has to be doing exactly the same thing at the same time. For example, if you are developing a skill such as passing the ball, you might want to change the distance over which pupils pass; thus groups passing over different distances will evolve naturally. Further, if you want to put pupils under greater pressure when practising passing, you might reduce the size of the playing area so that they have less time to make decisions. Conversely, you might extend the playing area, thereby increasing the space available as well as the time in which decisions can be made.

Consideration also needs to be given to the roles that pupils undertake. If you refer back to Chapter 3, the Sport Education model provides specific roles and responsibilities. The integration of these into the learning environment may provide pupils with increased levels of responsibility and can enhance BESD.

We can also look at the ways in which pupils interact with each other. As has previously been identified, many pupils with SEN will have associated communication needs. Consequently you will need to consider the opportunities you provide for pupils to communicate either with each other or with you as the teacher. You may need to think about the questions you ask, the time you give pupils to respond, as well as to whom they respond. Is it necessary for them to talk to the whole class, or will sharing answers in small groups be more appropriate?

Presentation

When looking at the way we present the lesson, we need to consider the way the lesson is structured (see Chapter 3 for the range of teaching styles that can be adopted); the responses that are expected from pupils (this may be the questions that will be asked, the answers expected, or in physical education the practice opportunities and demonstrations you might be planning); the resources you are intending to use (in physical education this may be more than just practical equipment for example they may include resources or reciprocal cards or ICT equipment); and any additional support that may be provided (many pupils with identified learning difficulties may have an assigned teaching assistant to support them in lessons).

Chapter 3 looked extensively at the teaching approaches and styles that can be adopted within lessons. If you have not read that chapter for some time, it might be worthwhile revisiting it. It is important to identify the objectives of your lesson and the most appropriate approach to adopt. Looking back at the domains of learning (see Chapters 2 and 3) may provide you with further guidance in these areas.

When looking at the responses that you are expecting from pupils, consideration needs to be given to how questions are introduced and the depth of response you are expecting. A range of questioning strategies can be used. You may ask closed questions where a specific answer is required, for example, 'do you understand?' which would elicit a yes or no response, or 'give me three teaching points for passing the ball'. While there may be more than three teaching points available you have been very specific in what you are looking for. Alternatively you could ask open-ended questions which give pupils the opportunity to give a range of responses. For example, 'how many different ways of passing a ball can you think of?' You can get pupils to expand their answers by asking them why they have chosen to do something in a certain way.

It is important to consider the ways in which pupils are encouraged to respond. For example, how can you ensure they will all be able to give a response? We have identified throughout this chapter aspects of giving pupils time to provide answers by thinking about when questions are asked, and when a response is expected. However, other strategies can include 'no hands up'. In such a strategy you are providing an opportunity for all pupils to provide a response as you identify the person from whom the response should come. In such a way you can gauge the first question (for example, a closed question) and then ask supplementary questions (open questions) to allow other pupils to expand on the first response.

If pupils are struggling to answer a question you might modify the question being asked, or alternatively provide them with 'help' strategies. For example, you might ask pupils to identify someone in the class they want to ask for help ('phone a friend'), they might pass the question over to someone else or they might 'ask the audience'. Such strategies are common in many games shows, but provide support mechanisms for pupils thereby limiting the impact of getting the question wrong. What is important is to establish a learning environment where it is acceptable to make mistakes; after all much of what we have learnt throughout our lives came as a result of getting something wrong in the first place!

The resources that are to be used are also important. In physical education our resources tend to be associated with the equipment we use, so we may want to think about the activity we are delivering and whether the equipment can be modified to ensure that all pupils achieve success. For example, when playing a racquet sport (tennis, badminton) can we use racquets with shorter handles to improve hand–eye co-ordination? Can we use racquets with large heads, so that there is a greater surface area with which to make contact with the ball or shuttle? Does the ball or shuttle have to be of a normal size, or can enlarged versions be used? When looking at introducing throwing or catching, can balls of different shapes and sizes be used? These are just a few examples of how equipment may be modified to support learning. More detail is included in Chapter 8, which looks at planning, and Chapters 6 and 7, which focus on the development of fundamental and activity specific skills.

However, the resources we use may not necessarily be restricted to equipment. Within physical education we may also use word walls or resource cards. It is therefore important to look at how these are developed and utilised within the context of the lesson.

The way we support learning within the physical education classroom is another important consideration. Many pupils with identified learning needs will be assigned a measure of support. This may include a designated staff member who accompanies pupils to lessons. It is important, if a pupil in your class is accompanied, that you provide adequate guidance to the staff member enabling them to provide the support that you require. This might involve meeting with them prior to the lesson to provide a brief overview of their role. You will be conscious of this process anyway as a result of your use of teaching assistants within your classroom-based lessons.

The support you provide may come from other pupils within your class. If you refer back to Chapter 2 and the theories of learning, you will remember that Vygotsky highlighted the use of peers to support learning. If you look at the teaching approaches identified by both Mosston and Ashworth (1994) and Metzler (2005), they too identified the use of peers to support learning. It is therefore important that if you are using such approaches clear guidance and structures are identified to ensure pupils are clear about their expectations and roles.

Content

The final group of strategies identified by Bailey (2006) around differentiation are associated with the content of the lesson. Specifically we are looking at:

- the tasks set
- the pace of the lesson
- the level at which pupils are being expected to work
- the style of practice being used.

You will be familiar with setting differentiated tasks within your classroom-based lessons. For example, you may group your class by ability represented by the tables they sit at, so that when setting work different tables are assigned different tasks. This practice is equally appropriate for physical education. Thinking back once more to the discussion of child development in Chapter 2, you will remember that different pupils will progress at different rates, and therefore setting the same task for all pupils may result in it being too easy for some pupils and too difficult for others. You need to be clear about the purpose of the task, and what you want pupils to get out of it. Earlier in this chapter we looked at the different way in which we ask questions of pupils and also the ways in which they may respond. It may be that while we may set a similar task for pupils, the outcome we are expecting from them is different. What is crucial here is that the pupils are fully aware of what outcome is expected.

The pace of a lesson refers to the speed at which the lesson progresses. It is a difficult skill to master. At times you will rush through things to ensure that you complete all the activities you have planned, while at other times you may move through the activities too slowly. The key here is to watch the class. They will send signals out as to whether they have completed the task, and therefore are starting to go off-task, or are struggling and therefore not fulfilling the requirements of the task. Both instances will require some form of intervention from you as the teacher. It may be that you need to refocus the group, move them on to the next task, or simplify the activity. Again this needs to be considered within your planning. Whatever you choose to do, you must be confident that it reflects the needs of the pupils. Do not be afraid to have different groups working on different tasks at different times. You do it all the time in the classroom! Organisationally it may also support you. For example, if one group has already completed the initial practice to the level you expect, move them onto the next practice. After completing the new practice they can then demonstrate to other groups what you want them to move on to. In this way you do not have to spend as much time explaining, thereby increasing the levels of activity within the lesson.

When we refer to the level of the activity we are making reference to the levels of attainment pupils are working at or towards. While there have been many changes to the content and organisation of the National Curriculum, there has been less change to the levels of attainment (see Chapter 1). Thus when looking at the content of the lesson, you need to also think about what level of attainment you are expecting. This may be written into the learning objectives set (see Chapter 8). Again consideration will need to be given to the range of levels you are addressing. Equally you will need to think carefully about how you might inform pupils of the levels at which they are working. This might be through identifying specific skills they must achieve for each level, remembering of course that in terms of the National Curriculum levels are not just associated with the skills they can perform, but also their levels of understanding and ability to communicate. It may well be that the tasks you set already reflect the different levels of attainment, or that the task set can be achieved through the demonstration of different skills reflective of different levels of attainment. This is particularly relevant if the tasks are of a very open-ended nature, as discussed earlier in the chapter.

Finally we look at the style of practice being used. Specifically we are looking at the ways in which the skills are practised. For example, would it be most appropriate for pupils to practise the skill on their own, with a partner or in a small group? How will they gain feedback about their performance – from each other, from you as the teacher, from watching their own performances using video?

While Bailey (2006) gives a detailed overview of differentiation across physical education, alternative models also exist. Youth Sport Trust (2004) and more recently TDA (2009) identify four key aspects of differentiation:

- **space:** this relates to the space (area) in which the activity is being performed – do you need to change it depending on the ability of the pupils?
- **task:** the activity you are asking the pupils to perform
- **equipment:** what the pupils are using to complete the task – do you need to modify the equipment they are being asked to use?
- **people:** who do you want the pupils to work with?

 Task 4.5

1 Using the previous section of the chapter, identify a range of differentiation strategies that you wish to try within your lessons.
2 For each strategy identify:

   a the activity you plan to deliver
   b the differentiation activities
   c how you will gauge the level of success.

3 Ask you school mentor colleague to observe the lessons in which you have planned to use these strategies and provide feedback to you on the outcomes of the approaches.

Chapter summary

The aim of this chapter has been to look at the range of individual needs evident within education and more specifically in the context of physical education. Further examples of differentiation and support strategies can be found on the companion website.

To summarise your learning in this chapter you may benefit from reflecting on the following review questions.

1   What is the range of SEN within the school environment?
2   How do these impact on the teaching of physical education?
3   How can differentiation be used to support these needs within a physical education context?
4   What key areas of personal development can you identify to increases your knowledge and understanding of these concepts?

Further reading

Bailey, R. (2006) *Teaching physical education: a handbook for primary and secondary school teachers*. London: Routledge.
While this book focuses on the delivery of physical education as a whole, Chapter 7 looks in more detail at SEN and how lessons can be differentiated to support pupil learning.

Teacher Development Agency (2009) *Including pupils with SEN and/or disabilities in primary physical education*. Manchester: TDA. Available at www.tda.gov.uk/school-leader/school-improvement/sen-and-disability/sen-training-resources/one-year-itt-programmes/~/media/resources/teacher/sen/primary/physical educationpe.pdf (accessed September 2011).
This publication provides guidance on supporting pupils with SEN within the context of physical education.

Smith, A. and Thomas, N. (2005) 'Inclusion, special educational needs, disability and physical education' in K. Green, and K. Hardman (eds), *Physical education: essential issues*. London: Sage. pp. 180–96.
This chapter provides an overview of issues associated with the engagement of pupils with specific needs within the physical education curriculum.

Relevant journals

Autism
Published bi-monthly this international and peer-reviewed journal provides practical help in the support of pupils with autism. Available at www.aut.sagepub.com (accessed September 2011).

Emotional and Behavioural Difficulties
Published four times a year, this journal provides practical support and guidance when working with pupils who have difficulties with BESD. Available at www.tandf.co.uk/journals/EBD (accessed September 2011).

Other useful websites

I CAN Talk series – www.ican.org.uk
Teacher Expertise – www.teachingexpertise.com

Organisations

Social Emotional and Behavioural Difficulties Association (SEBDA) – www.sebda.org

I CAN – charity set up to support children with communication needs. Their associated website www.ican.org.uk provides support and guidance aimed at the development and improvement of communication skills.

CHAPTER 5

SAFE PRACTICE IN PHYSICAL EDUCATION

Chapter aims

- To develop an understanding of what pupils need to know about health and safety in the context of physical education
- To identify issues associated with specific areas of activity, including warming up and cooling down
- To develop an understanding of the processes associated with the assessment of risk
- To develop an understanding of aspects of classroom and behaviour management specific to physical education

Central to the learning experiences in physical education is the need to create a safe environment, where pupils feel able to contribute effectively across a range of activities. Consideration needs to be given to the organisation and management of the learning environment in respect of safety issues associated not only with specific activities, for example athletic activities and OAA, but also with the organisation of equipment and learning spaces. We also need to look at health and safety associated with warming up and cooling down, so that pupils can engage fully with the learning activities.

In order to assess your own current level of understanding associated with safe practice in physical education, read and complete Task 5.1.

 Task 5.1

1 Using the six areas of activity identified in Chapter 1 and your existing knowledge, produce a table identifying what you feel are the key safety issues that need to be planned for within physical education.
2 Produce a checklist that you can use during the planning process to take account of the issues you have identified.

What pupils need to know about health and safety in a physical education context

It is important that everyone is involved in the management of safe practice, including the pupils you teach. Within general teaching requirements (explored in more detail in Chapter 9) there is an expectation that pupils will be taught about health and safety in education. In any teaching environment, pupils need to have a clear understanding of how their behaviours and actions may impact on their own and others, health and safety. This might include how they collect, return and move equipment as well as aspects of behaviour related to playing specific games. They need to understand the specific risks associated with individual activities in order to think about how these can be reduced. In essence pupils need to develop an understanding of risks and how they can be involved in the control and management of these. Task 5.2 requires you to think about some of the strategies you might employ to develop pupils' understanding of these within your lessons.

 Task 5.2

1 Identify a set of key behaviours you expect pupils to demonstrate within your lessons, for example:

   a how they enter and leave your lesson
   b how they collect and return equipment
   c what they should wear
   d how they behave when getting changed.

2 For each activity provide a simple rationale for why they should behave in these ways.
3 Produce a set of resource cards which can be displayed in your classroom so that pupils know and understand what these behaviours are (you could ask pupils to produce these themselves to allow them to develop a deeper understanding).

Health and safety across areas of activity

Common principles

In many respects health and safety procedures reflect common sense. Common principles can be applied to all activities focusing on the facilities and equipment being used, what pupils are expected to wear (including footwear), the organisation of the activities being taught and staff competence to teach the specific skills. Table 5.1 provides an overview of the key principles that can be applied across areas of activity.

Each activity will have contextual safety issues which we will explore in more detail as we move through this chapter, but generic principles are also evident, and we will look at these in more detail now.

Whitlam and Beaumont (2008) identify the following common principles of safe practice:

- knowledge of the activity being taught
- knowledge of developmental processes
- knowledge of first aid
- knowledge of behaviour and classroom management strategies
- safeguarding pupils.

Knowledge of the activity being taught

As the teacher, you should have a sound level of knowledge and understanding of the activities that you are teaching. This should include appropriate warm-up

Table 5.1 Common principles in healthy and safe practice

Facilities	Are they fit for purpose? Are they well maintained? Are playing/working surfaces safe?
Equipment	Is it fit for purpose? Is it well maintained? How will it be distributed and collected? Does it need to be moved in a specific manner?
Clothing/footwear	Is it appropriate for the activity? Is there a risk of it snagging on any equipment? Are trainers tied appropriately? Is the footwear appropriate for the activity being taught?
Pupils	Is long hair tied back? Is jewellery removed? Are there any medical conditions affecting pupils?
Teachers and adults other than teachers	Do they have appropriate qualifications?
Planning and organisation	Are lessons appropriately planned taking into account the age and ability of pupils?

and cool-down activities, the skills that need to be taught and the rules that apply to the activity.

During your initial teacher education you will receive or have received a general introduction to aspects of teaching physical education. You may feel that the amount of time spent learning about physical education does not always provide adequate depth of knowledge or sufficient opportunity to practise these skills during teaching placements. It is therefore important during your initial and early professional development that, when you are teaching a new activity or an activity that you have not taught for some time, you read up on the activity and its associated risks (a list of activity specific websites can be found on the companion website to support you with this). If you have any doubts about your ability to teach the activity then you could to talk to and observe a more experienced teacher, or engage in professional development opportunities such as attending coaching courses run within your local area.

Knowledge of developmental processes

You should have an understanding of the developmental processes in physical education and the activities pupils can be expected to perform at the different stages of development. These are often referred to as 'developmentally appropriate activities' (Chapters 6 and 7 look at these in more detail). As well as thinking about the progression of the activities to be taught, you also need to have an understanding of the pupils in your group, for example do any of them have SEN and how will you manage these? You might wish to refer back to Chapters 2 and 4 at this point. How this is then reflected in the planning of the learning episode is covered in Chapter 8. It is important that pupils are not expected to do activities that are too developmentally challenging and which require skills they have not had the opportunity to develop. We also need to give consideration to the perceived risk – that is the risk that pupils may perceive to exist in an activity they may regard as too challenging – and the actual risk involved. This tends to be lower than that which is perceived. This is very common in OAA and we will follow this up later in the chapter.

Knowledge of first aid

Knowledge of basic first aid is advantageous, and this should be supported with a clear understanding of the medical procedures and policies in place where you are employed or at the facilities that you might use to deliver physical education, for example local sport centres or local swimming pools. You should ensure that you know if any of your pupils have a medical condition (asthma is the most common) and that they have their medication with them (this should be labelled, especially if they are giving them to you for safe keeping). If you are taking pupils off site for extra-curricular activities, running practices out of school hours or taking them on residential trips, consent forms should be completed which clearly identify any potential medical conditions.

Knowledge of behaviour and classroom management strategies

You should have a sound knowledge of behaviour and classroom management strategies. These will be similar to those procedures already in place within your lessons, allowing pupils to understand that expected behaviours are common across subject areas. Pupils should be clear about what constitutes acceptable and unacceptable behaviour (you may well have developed this during the completion of Task 5.2). Rewards and sanctions should be applied consistently in line with school policy. In some cases you might develop sanctions which reflect practice within sporting activities, for example issuing a green card as a warning about behaviour (commonly used in hockey), a yellow card which reflects sin-binning resulting in time out of the activity (used in rugby) or a red card when pupils are removed from the activity (used in football).

Most behaviour issues within a lesson stem from times when pupils are off task and no longer engaged in a focused learning activity. Task 5.3 requires you to start looking at this in more detail.

 Task 5.3: Behaviour management

1 From your experiences identify a range of opportunities for off-task behaviour to occur.
2 For each opportunity identify a series of strategies you might use to reduce the impact of these opportunities.

Having completed Task 5.3 you will have identified some major 'problem points' where off-task behaviour may occur. Table 5.2 identifies a number of off-task opportunities and potential strategies that can be used to reduce their impact.

Safeguarding pupils

As the teacher it is your responsibility to create a safe and effective learning environment. You will be aware of the safety checks which are undertaken when you embark on initial teacher education programmes and when you take up your first post or engage in working with young people. There is a responsibility for schools to ensure that any individual working with pupils has similar checks undertaken.

Table 5.2 Strategies for managing behaviour

Opportunity	Strategy
Arriving and departing from the lesson	Require pupils to line up prior to entering the lesson Have a controlled entry into the changing areas
Changing – before and after the lesson	Provide a designated changing area for each pupil, for example: • boys change in one areas, girls in another Be clear what pupils do once they have changed, for example: • spare clothing is folded and left on their chair if changing in a classroom • pupils sit on the carpet area when they are changed Play a piece of music by the end of which all pupils should be ready to start the lesson
Moving between the changing and teaching space	Pupils walk in silence between the areas

Collecting, moving with, distributing and returning equipment	Designate specific pupils to collect equipment (this can be done when they are sitting on the carpet area at the start of the lesson)
	Limit the number of pupils collecting equipment for specific activities
	
	• Number pupils and have only one pupil per group collecting equipment
	• This can be repeated to return equipment
	• Be very specific about how equipment should be moved
	• How gymnastic equipment should be carried
	   ◦ Number of pupils
	   ◦ Lifting techniques

Changing of activities	• Limit the number of changes to activities • Be clear about how much information pupils need to be given for each task • Change the activity one group at a time so that you are not calling them all in at the same time • Ask pupils to leave equipment in their working space so they are not 'playing' with it as you try to explain the next task

Safeguarding pupils means much more than vetting who is teaching a pupil. It means ensuring that pupils feel safe in the environment they are working in. This includes their physical, emotional, social and personal well-being. Chapter 10 looks at this aspect in more depth, focusing on the use of external providers.

Consideration should also be given to the recording and use of images of pupils. Chapter 9 looks at how ICT skills can be developed through the use of videoing performances which are then reviewed to provide feedback. Clear guidelines need to be adhered to regarding how these images are then stored or deleted. Your school will be able to provide further details about their specific policies and practices.

This first section has looked at the generic principles and issues associated with creating and maintaining a safe environment for learning. The next section looks in more detail at the principles associated with warming up and cooling down in physical education.

Warming up and cooling down in physical education

Pupils need to develop an understanding of the principles associated with preparing for and recovering from physical activity. Some of the pupils you teach will participate in physical activity away from the school environment and may experience different approaches. This may be beneficial for you as the teacher as you can encourage them to support you when warming up the rest of the class, but you yourself should be clear as to what activities should be included.

A warm up provides the opportunity for pupils to prepare their bodies for the activities they are expected to perform during the lesson. Therefore the activities included within the warm up should be closely aligned to those planned for during the lesson. Initial activities should be low intensity, for example walking or slow jogging, which starts to increase the heart rate. During this period, pupils can start to think about what is happening to their body as they are warming up (this is covered in more detail in Chapter 9). Sport-specific warm-up activities can then be introduced, for example activities that encourage a change in speed or direction as you would encounter in games activities. At this point equipment relevant to the activity can also be introduced. Once the muscles have warmed up, stretching activities can be introduced. These should be performed in a static position where the stretch is held for 6–10 seconds (Youth Sports Trust and Central YMCA, 1998). What is important after the warm up is that pupils remain active, which will require you to think about how you make the transition from the warm-up to the first activity.

When cooling down the emphasis is on returning the body to a resting level. You should move from energetic to more sedate activities requiring the body to work at ever decreasing speeds. The format is similar to the warm up culminating in static stretching; however, this time stretches should be held for longer.

A range of warming-up and cooling-down activities can be found on the companion website including games and stretching. The section on further reading also identifies additional literature you may wish to access.

Activity specific safety considerations

Athletic activities

Chapter 7 looks at specific areas of activity relating to athletics. Consideration needs to be given to the organisation and management of the working area and equipment being used as well as the pupils being taught.

Within the school environment, the teaching of athletic activities takes place either on the school field or the school playground. Consideration needs to be given to the surface being used, for example whether the grass is dry enough.

Even in the height of the summer early morning lessons may be affected by dew on the grass causing it to be slippery and limiting activities such as throwing and jumping. Playground surfaces can also be affected by dampness as well as the build-up of grit, which presents a skid hazard. Below are key considerations you should plan for in throwing lessons. Table 5.3 provides a basic checklist for you to consider when planning other lessons.

Table 5.3   Checklist for health and safety considerations in athletic activities

Jumping	Throwing	Running
Is the area free from foreign objects? Is the jumping surface dry? Are the facilities and equipment being used fit for purpose?	Has a designated throwing area been identified? Do pupils fully understand the rules regarding the activity including: • when to throw • when to collect? Is the throwing area dry and free from foreign objects? Are the pupils appropriately spaced?	Are the facilities and equipment being used fit for purpose?

The spacing of pupils during throwing activities

Pupils need to be placed a sufficient distance apart to ensure that during the release of the object they are not going to hit anyone else. This does not mean that all pupils have to throw from the same point one after the other, but it does require you to consider whether pupils throw at the same time, or in sequence. It is important that pupils move backwards once they have thrown. Not only is this one of the rules associated with throwing events (in that they must not step out of the front of the throwing area), but it also prevents pupils throwing and then walking out to collect at the same time as others may still be throwing. The easiest way to do this is to use cones to identify throwing areas, waiting areas and observation areas.

In order to increase levels of activity, a specified throwing area can be designated in the shape of a circle or fan (see Figure 5.1). Using such an approach, which can also be used in the teaching of striking skills in games activities allows a higher level of interaction.

The hand from which the object is thrown

It would seem logical that if a pupil is throwing right-handed the flight path of the object will be different to that of objects thrown from the left hand. Consideration therefore needs to be given to where pupils stand in relation to others.

How the thrown object is collected

In many respects the teaching of throwing activities is best controlled in the first instance through the use of direct teaching approaches, overseen by you as the teacher (see Chapter 3). Pupils are directed when to throw the object,

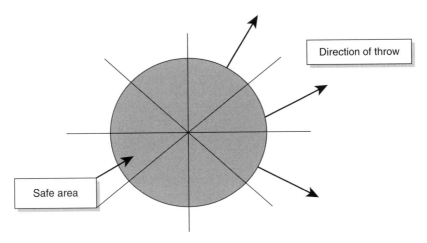

Figure 5.1 Throwing area in the shape of a circle or fan

Adapted from Youth Sport Trust (2004) TOP Play and TOP Sport Student Handbook – Using TOP Play and TOP Sport in higher education institutions, section 5, p 18.

normally being told when to do so. There is a tendency post-throw for pupils to walk out to collect their object. This is very dangerous particularly if others have yet to throw. Once pupils have thrown, they should return to the safe area which allows them to receive feedback from their partner about their perform-ance, after which their partner or they should go and collect the object under the control of the teacher.

Dance activities

When delivering dance activities, generic principles of health and safety should be addressed. These include ensuring that effective warm-up opportunities are planned for and delivered and that when specific techniques are required these are taught effectively and reflect the developmental maturity of pupils. Consideration also needs to be given to the facilities being used. In a primary school dance is likely to be taught in the school hall. If you draw a picture of your hall it probably includes a piano, seating, gymnastics equipment and din-ing tables. While this does not prevent the effective teaching of dance, consid-eration needs to be given to isolating these objects so that pupils do not climb or jump onto them, and so that they do not fall. You also need to ensure that the floor is clean and dry, especially after lunch.

Games activities

Consideration needs to be given to the playing surface, specifically to whether it is free from foreign objectives, for example litter. This is particularly important if your field is open to public access. Playgrounds should be free from grit. Equipment should be developmentally appropriate, for example in hockey the sticks should be the right size for the pupils. You may need to consider using softer balls when introducing throwing and catching skills.

When establishing playing areas you will need to consider the size, as well as location in relation to other playing areas. You might want to provide grid areas either designated with line markings or the use of cones (further examples of this are included in Chapters 6 and 7). This limits pupils from running into each other's games. You will also need to think about where equipment is located and stored during activities, particularly if it is not in use.

Gymnastic activities

Health and safety issues when teaching gymnastic activities focus on the facilities and the equipment being used. The nature of the activities taught in gymnastics requires the use of different pieces of equipment, for example mats, benches, movement tables, wall bars. Mats need to be stored correctly so mat trolleys should be used which require mats to be stored flat or held in a vertical position. When placed on the floor the mats should be flat to avoid a trip hazard. They should be free of holes and, as with all gymnastic equipment, they should be checked and serviced regularly. Gymnastic equipment is not cheap, and therefore pupils should be taught how to look after it in regard to its storage, carriage and use.

Benches should sit flat on the floor and you should avoid placing them on mats which can cause them to rock. If using wooden benches, these need to be free of splinters and varnished regularly. Foam-topped benches need to be checked for holes which may cause a reduction in the padding. When using benches, consideration also needs to be given to the location of mats around them. A mat will tend to indicate an exit point off the equipment and this can be used to control movement around the equipment. However, a mat can also be interpreted as a landing point, and therefore you will need to be very clear about whether pupils can jump off the equipment.

Movement tables raise similar issues as benches. They offer the potential to increase the height at which skills are performed and therefore you will need to specify how you expect pupils to exit the piece of equipment. This is particularly important when jumping off.

As with all equipment, wall bars need regular servicing. Activities taught using wall bars encourage the use of height so depending on the age of pupils you may consider limiting the height which they are allowed to climb.

Outdoor and adventurous activities

If teaching OAA, such as orienteering and basic problem solving in schools, the same generic principles associated with health and safety apply. Consideration needs to be given to the location of the teacher in relation to the pupils doing the activity. You need to be confident that you can be seen by the pupils in your class as much as possible, but also need to have some form of signal should you need them to return to the lesson base at any point. When completing problem-solving activities, consideration needs to be given to the equipment being used, as well as the surfaces on which the activities are being completed.

If you are involved in residential-based activities you will need to have a detailed knowledge and understanding of the potential risks associated with each activity. While the instructors delivering the sessions will have responsibility for the specific activities, you will still be expected to reinforce expectations around behaviour management. You may find that you take responsibility for activities during the evenings and you should make sure that you fully understand any safety procedures that need to be adhered to.

Swimming-based activities

In swimming-based activities you need to ensure pupils understand how to behave appropriately in and around the pool. For example, pupils will need to learn appropriate behaviours associated with changing, moving around the area, for example by not running, and entering and exiting the pool (see the companion website for further details). You will need to understand the roles and responsibilities of different individuals involved in the delivery of swimming, as well as how pupils travel to and from the pool and how they are monitored in the changing rooms. There is also a need to reflect upon the organisation of the learning environment in which pupils will be working.

Assessing risk

When embarking on any activity for the first time, you should undertake a risk assessment. This process requires you to look at the activity and assess potential problems (risks) and how you intend to reduce the potential for them to occur, and consider any actions you might need to take. Each school will have a policy and staff member with overall responsibility for the co-ordination of these assessments. It is important that you also apply these to any external facilities that you might use. Examples of risk assessments can be found on the companion website.

Chapter summary

This chapter provides a brief overview of the key principles associated with safe practice in physical education. To consolidate your learning you should now spend some time completing the review questions below.

1 What are the key principles associated with the safe delivery of effective physical education lessons?
2 For each of the six activity areas, identify a set of rules you would expect your pupils to adhere to.
3 Produce risk assessments for a range of the activities you teach – add these to your portfolio.

Further reading

Harris, J. and Elbourn, J. (2002) *Warming up and cooling down.* Leeds: Human Kinetics.
This practical text offers a range of warm-up and cool-down activities appropriate for inclusion in physical education lessons.

Shaughnessy, J. (2008) 'Health and safety: guidelines to support teaching and learning in PE', in I. Pickup, L. Price, J. Shaughnessy, J. Spence and M. Trace (eds), *Learning to teaching primary PE*. Exeter: Learning Matters. pp. 87–108.
This chapter focuses on the range of issues associated with delivering safe learning experiences.

Whitlam, P. and Beaumont, G. (eds) (2008) *Safe practice in physical education and school sport*. Leeds: Coachwise Ltd.
Written specifically for physical education practitioners this comprehensive text provides specific guidance across activity areas and sports. It also provides general guidance on areas such as competence, curriculum management, use of facilities, off-site activities and safeguarding pupils.

CHAPTER 6

DEVELOPING MOTOR COMPETENCES

Chapter aims

- To develop an understanding of the principles of motor competences in physical education
- To develop an understanding of the fundamental motor skills relevant to physical education
- To develop an understanding of motor development in pupils

Chapter 2 introduced principles of child development predominantly focusing on learning. The aim of this chapter is to look in detail at the fundamental motor skills that pupils should develop from the ages of 3 to 11. We also consider a range of developmental activities that can be integrated into lesson planning in order to emphasise key teaching points associated with skill development.

Developing early motor skills

According to Gallahue and Ozmun (1995) and QCDA (2010a) three discrete stages of motor development occur: the initial or early, the elementary or middle and the mature or late. In contrast, Physical Education Association of the United Kingdom (PEAUK) (2003) identify two stages: the early and late motor pattern. These developmental stages, however they are constructed, include different motor skills, and the development of these skills will be reflected to some extent in the curriculum, both in England and in other countries.

Most of the pupils with whom you work will already have experienced a wealth of developmental opportunities during the early stages of their development as a result of their interactions with different individuals or environments. They will have started to develop basic motor skills associated with stability (balance), locomotion (movement) and manipulation (use of hands). These concepts will therefore underpin any physical work in the Foundation Stage and early years of primary education.

 Task 6.1

1 From your current experience, what would you regard as the fundamental motor skills pupils should learn?
2 Why do you think these are important?
3 Do you think there is any specific order in which they should be developed?

Current resources for the development of early motor skills focus on fundamental skills (see physicaleducationresources.com) and on a multi-skills approach to physical education (see Raising the Bar at www.creativedevelopment.co.uk/tag/raising-the-bar), for the 0–7 age range.

What emerges from the available literature and resources is a generic approach to developing fundamental skills through engaging pupils in a range of activities, underpinned by a guiding principle that children need these basic skills for lifelong participation in physical education and physical activity. What we as teachers therefore need to do is to understand these specific skills and identify activities that can be used to support their development.

The range of supporting resources currently available demonstrates not only the recent investment in physical education, but also an increased awareness of the need to support those who work with pupils during the early stages of their development (www.youthsportdirect.org.uk provides examples of such resources). Such resources build upon the work of researchers looking at growth and development within the physical domain (see Chapter 2 for more detail). The progressive nature of skill development is a common theme within this literature. In the early stages of development we concentrate on basic motor skills and concepts rather than expecting pupils to engage in more complex games and activities. As a consequence the remainder of this chapter will focus on the development of generic skills rather than on specific games or activities (examples of these can be found on the companion website). This will demonstrate the inter-relatedness of many of the skills discussed.

A common classification of fundamental skills used by physical education practitioners is ABC (Agility, Balance and Co-ordination) (Sports Coach UK). This categorisation has been used to produce a Multi-Skills Club of resources and activities designed to develop pupils' competences within these areas (Youth Sport Trust – www.youthsporttrust.org.uk). In a similar vein, national governing bodies of sport have also started to develop FUNdamental resources (British Gymnastics), which are designed to support learning activities that not only develop basic motor skills, but are also enjoyable for children.

As well as these ABC skills we should also look at the categories of motor skills which include locomotion, core stability and those involving some form of manipulation (see Table 6.1).

Table 6.1 Categories of motor skills

Locomotion	Stability	Manipulation
Walk	Bend	Throw
Run	Stretch	Catch
Leap	Reach	Kick
Hop	Twist	Trap
Jump	Turn	Roll
Slide		Strike
Gallop		Volley
Rotation		Write
		Construct

 Task 6.2

1 Using Table 6.1, reflect upon the skills identified.
2 What knowledge do you have of performing these skills?
3 What do you feel are the key teaching points for each of these skills?
4 You may wish to develop a resource file to collate the tasks completed in this chapter so that you can use them in your teaching.

Looking at the skills listed above, you will appreciate that fundamental motor skills are those which we take for granted in any activities we engage in, and form the basis for any physical education that we might participate in as adults. For example, we run in many games-based activities, in athletics, in dance and in gymnastics, as a means of developing our fitness. We turn when we change direction in games-based activities, in gymnastics and in dance. We throw in games activities, in aquatic activities and in athletic activities. When we view skill development in this way, we can begin to acknowledge the inter-related nature of skills in physical education.

Fundamental motor skills

We can divide fundamental motor skills into skills that focus on specific body parts. One of the simplest ways to do this is a top-down approach to the human body, for instance by thinking about what the head is doing, what the arms are doing, what the main body is doing, and finally what the legs and feet do (PEAUK, 2003). This allows us to observe performances in detail, avoiding the opportunity to give focused and specific feedback. The next section of the chapter focuses on specific skills.

Locomotor skills

You may wish to refer back to Table 6.1 for a complete overview of the different locomotor skills.

Running

Running is the basic movement that allows us to cover ground at speed, and the speed at which we run will vary depending upon the activity. For example, if we are running to develop our fitness then we are likely to travel at a gentle pace over a longer period of time, while in many activities we undertake within physical education we will run at speed. In essence a run is an extension of a walk, so the adage that 'you can't run before you can walk' is indeed correct.

With any skill key teaching or learning points can be used to guide the performer as well as providing a framework through which feedback about performances can be given. When developing the skill of running the following points should be focused upon.

- Teaching point 1: The head must remain as still as possible with the eyes focused upon a point in the direction of travel – when learning to run it can be common for children to rotate the head from side to side, and this rotation can lead to a lack of co-ordination and balance in the upper body (torso and shoulders). A further common fault occurs as a result of the learner focusing their gaze towards the floor leading to forward rotation of the body. An easy way to think about how this would feel is to imagine yourself running very quickly down a hill and the lack of balance and co-ordination you would feel when doing this. An easy way to address this is to get children to identify a spot on the horizon or wall of the hall and focus on that when running.
- Teaching point 2: Arms and legs work in opposition – this may seem self-explanatory, but that is because this is a skill that we perform habitually, without really thinking about it. If a pupil is performing the skill with the

same arm and leg moving at the same time, you will see a lot of body rotation (you might find it useful to have a go at running in this way to fully understand). The key to this teaching point is to encourage the learner to relax and do what comes naturally. You could start any activity at walking pace, and as pupils' confidence and competence develop encourage them to increase the pace at which they are working.

- Teaching point 3: Arms pump by your side rather than across the body which results in upper body rotation – again this teaching point is better appreciated if you have a go at doing it yourself. While standing on the spot pump your arms as though you are running, but rather than your arms going forwards and backwards, move your arms across your body so that your right hand finishes across the left side of your body and your left arm finishes across your right side. What you should feel is that your torso rotates. Now try the same practice with your right and left hands finishing pointing forward. Can you feel the difference?
- Teaching point 4: Upper body leans forward – as the first teaching point was that we should encourage learners to look straight ahead, leaning forward while running could seem contradictory; however, a slight forward lean will enhance balance.

What activities can we use to encourage skill development? With the running-related activities discussed above it is sensible at first to encourage pupils to perform the skill on the spot. As they become more confident they can start to perform the skill at walking pace and over time increase their speed. If they are struggling to run in a straight line you can encourage them to follow a line on the ground, or provide them with two cones to run between. To develop agility you can then get them to run round cones (slalom). You can consider setting up relay activities to encourage co-operative opportunities, although you need to be aware that as competition is introduced you may find that the skill level declines as children emphasise winning over following set techniques. You will also need to consider the learning environment you are creating by introducing competition (see Chapter 2 for more information on this).

Jumping

Jumping can be used across activities. As with running, the performance will be influenced by what we are trying to achieve. In jumping we might wish to jump for height, to catch a ball, or for distance in a long jump. However, when we look at jumping in gymnastics and dance-based activities, we can identify five different ways to jump:

- one foot to one foot (hop)
- one foot to the other (leap)
- two feet to one foot
- two feet to two feet
- one foot to two feet (hopscotch).

Again we can break the skill down to reflect what the body parts are doing.

If we look at the skill from the top down, we can start by thinking about what our head is doing. As with running, we want to encourage the learner to focus their eyes forward on a spot in front of them. This ensures that they are not looking at their feet and avoids unnecessary forward rotation. We then need to focus on the arms and legs. It is important that children bend their knees to provide power for the take-off, and bend them again when landing to absorb the impact. You may already know that the knee joint is sometimes referred to as a hinge joint. If the knees are not bent on landing, then the shock-absorbing mechanisms of the joint will not function, resulting in shock waves (a jolting sensation) being experienced throughout the body. Over time this may cause an injury.

While the legs act as the power behind the skill, the arms also contribute. Depending on the purpose of the jump, the arms will act differently. If you are encouraging jumping for height, the arms will swing forward and up; when jumping for distance the arms will swing forward and back. Practising this part of the skill standing still will allow you to feel the impact of the movement of the body.

In terms of setting suitable challenges to support skill development we can ask pupils to jump up and touch an object, for example a suspended balloon. This will encourage them to jump for height. If we are looking at encouraging them to jump for distance then we can ask them to jump forward to a cone. A fun challenge is to get them to predict how far they can jump and place a cone on the floor. Children can then try to reach this cone and either move it forward if they have passed it or backwards if they have not reached it. As they become more proficient they can be encouraged to jump over objects. As with all physical activities you will need to consider relevant aspects of health and safety, a topic discussed in greater depth in Chapter 5.

As your pupils' ability to perform basic jumps improves you can get them to think about the shapes their bodies make when in the air. For example, a straight jump requires them to jump up with their hands stretched above their heads, their fingers pointing up and their toes pointing towards the floor. A tuck jump requires them to jump up and bring their knees to their chest. Caution is suggested when introducing this skill as learners may have a tendency to bring their chest to meet their knees resulting in them forming a ball shape which will lead to a lack of stability.

Rotation

Rotation skills can be used to travel in both gymnastics and dance activities. Perhaps the easiest roll to perform is the log roll, also known as the pencil roll. The log roll requires pupils to lie on their backs flat on the floor. Hands and arms should be stretched up above the head with fingers pointed. Toes should be pointed towards the floor. If pupils are struggling to understand this, an easy way for them to get a feel for the position is to ask them to stand upright on their toes with their arms stretched up above their heads. You can also get them to link the starting position to how they perform a straight jump.

Pupils start by lying on the floor on their backs. The aim of the log roll is to rotate the body to either the left or the right, moving from lying on the back to lying on the stomach and then finishing on the back (see Figure 6.1). In order to achieve this, learners will need to form a shallow dish shape and rock slightly to the side to gain enough momentum to roll over.

A consideration when teaching this skill is the muscular development of the pupil, in particular around the neck region. Ideally the head should remain in-between the arms when the skill is performed. Those performing the skill at an early developmental stage, however, may lift their head so that it destabilises the movement. This has a resulting impact on the direction of travel. One way to address this is to encourage pupils to roll between two cones, or to place a cone on the ground above their fingers and another below their toes before they begin and then place a series of cones along their direction of travel to see how much they move off course. If using mats (see Chapter 5 for information on the safe use of equipment) they can use the side of the mat as a target.

Having looked at the three basic locomotor skills you might wish to think about how you would develop these within your own lessons. Task 6.3 gives you the opportunity to do this.

 Task 6.3

1 Observe either a lesson or a play-based session (this could include a break time).

   a Identify pupils performing basic locomotor skills.
   b Using the key teaching points identified for each skill, identify at what levels pupils are performing (for example, an early or a late motor pattern).
   c Identify how you might improve pupils' performance by including activities you might encourage pupils to participate in.

2 If you have the opportunity, provide feedback to those you have observed and revisit their skill at a later date to identify any progress that has been made.

Figure 6.1 The log roll

Stability skills

Stability skills encourage the development of control and co-ordination and are therefore closely aligned to the requirements of both early childhood documentation and Key Stage 1 development. As Table 6.1 identifies, the key skills are associated with bending, stretching, reaching, twisting and turning.

When looking at bending, stretching and reaching, we can see similarities in the activities we may encourage pupils to perform. When we think of bending we might consider the directions in which we might bend, for example forwards or to the side. We might consider bending as relating to stretching and therefore use bending activities during the warm-up aspect of our lesson (see Chapter 5 for developing warm-up activities and also the associated health and safety aspects of the activity). As with many locomotor skills, stability skills are core components of many types of activities.

As well as integrating such activities into the warm-up phase of the lesson, we can also develop focused activities within the main body of the lessons. Returning to bending, we can ask pupils to think about what parts of their body they can bend to form different shapes. This will encourage pupils to start thinking about what different body parts can do. For example, our body tends to bend predominantly from the middle, so we can bend to move toward our toes, and then reach up to go up on to our toes to make ourselves tall and thin. This is a good activity to encourage children to consider how they will feel when doing a straight jump, or equally what their starting point is for the log roll discussed in the previous section. We may also consider getting children to make shapes with their bodies lying on the floor, for example 'star shape'. Alternatively we could set the challenge of making as many different letters using their bodies, for example S, L, X, T, P, O, I. Such activities can then be developed into gymnastic or dance-based activities, for example over time pupils can be encouraged to repeat these movements using different pieces of equipment, or work with a partner to form different body shapes.

We need to think about how we can develop pupils' reaching skills. Again it is important that we think about the range of movements and activities that require some form of reaching. If we think about throwing and catching (covered in more detail later in this chapter) we reach to catch a ball. We could encourage pupils to reach up when performing a straight jump; equally we want pupils to reach up when starting the log roll.

Twisting and turning skills are not limited to gymnastic or dance-related activities; we might also turn to change direction, or twist when we try to move away from an opponent. If we think about a simple warm-up game such as 'Stuck in the mud' (if playing such games you will need to be very specific about how players are released, for example ensuring pupils move under the arms from front to back), pupils will be regularly required to twist and turn to avoid capture by the 'tagger'. If we are playing a game that requires pupils to change direction on command (see the companion website under the section on warm-up activities for a range of appropriate activities) it is likely that they will use twisting and turning activities.

We can develop twisting and turning activities using jumps, for example asking pupils to jump and turn to face the opposite wall thereby rotating 180 degrees. We can also consider developing twisting and turning movements to move along, on, off or over equipment. This can be developed by encouraging pupils to explore different ways of moving, or by giving them a range of movements that they can try.

Manipulation skills

Table 6.1 also identifies the range of manipulative skills we need to encourage during the early stages of development. These skills are used in activities which require pupils to use different body parts to hold, move, receive and send objects.

Rolling an object

Developing pupils' ability to roll a ball can be used as a precursor to developing the skills of throwing and catching. The benefit of introducing this skill early on is that it allows for the development of the basic characteristics of throwing and is performed in such a way as to encourage pupils' confidence in receiving a moving object. Many aspects associated with this skill can be performed in small areas and allow for the development of control as well as co-operative skills.

An effective way to roll an object would involve a pupil standing side-on to an intended target, although at the early stages of development pupils will tend to face the intended target, which restricts the amount of power that can be generated. The rolling hand should start extended backwards away from the body, and the opposite foot should be placed forward. The hand should end up pointing at the intended target, and this is a key teaching point for many skills used to send objects (see the section on throwing for a development of this concept).

When receiving a rolled ball the receiver should be positioned behind the ball, with their hands low to trap the ball.

In developing this skill, the following paired activities can be used.

1 Pupils lie on their stomachs facing their partner. They roll the ball to each other with the aim of trapping the ball in front of the chest. By lying on their stomachs, power is generated from the shoulders. Variations include:
   a using one hand, using both hands, using the non-preferred hand (the one they would not usually use to send the ball)
   b using different sized balls
   c placing two cones in between the pair to form a goal and challenging the participants to get the ball through the goal before it reaches their partner, – this encourages the development of directional skills and can be made more challenging by decreasing the size of the goal

      d increasing the distances the ball has to travel

      e challenging the pairs to see how many passes can be made in a specified time.

2 Pupils sit on the floor, their legs apart forming a V shape, opposite their partner. They roll the ball to their partner who aims to trap the ball in their hands. By being seated the power for the pass must come from the upper body. Variations to the activity can include those listed under the first activity.

3 Pupils stand opposite their partner and roll the ball to each other. The emphasis here is on developing pupils' abilities to use all parts of their bodies to generate power and control using the whole of the body. If you are working in clearly defined work areas, this activity can be developed to encourage movement. Instead of sending the ball directly to their partner, they could send the ball to the side of them so their partner changes position before receiving the ball.

Throwing

Throwing involves the sending of an object over a distance. When performed effectively this should demonstrate movement of the thrower's body from back foot to front foot using a stepping action where necessary. This is commonly known as weight transfer. A number of different throws can be performed (underarm, overarm, chest pass, bounce pass), although the principles for their effective performance are similar.

As with locomotor skills we can analyse throwing by looking at what different body parts do when performing this skill. A pupil performing a throwing action during the early stages of development will tend to stand facing the intended direction of the throw, and when releasing the ball will tend to rotate forward from the waist with a limited transference of weight. In developing this aspect of the skill, pupils should be encouraged to stand sideways on to the target with the opposite foot forward to their throwing hand, so if they are throwing with their right hand their left foot would be forward. You may wish to identify on the floor the position of their feet using cones, chalk marks or even feet shapes. The sideways stance will allow pupils to step forward, thereby transferring their weight from back to front and giving power to their throw.

Having looked at general body position we will now turn to the arms. Arms and hands contribute power and direction to throwing. If we think back to the basic biomechanical principles learnt during science lessons, we will remember that the body is made up of a series of joints. The elbow is known as a hinge joint, allowing movement in general forwards and backwards. The other major arm joint is located at the shoulder. This ball and socket joint allows much more movement, including a capacity for rotation. As the ability to throw develops there is a change from the predominant use of the elbow joint, which will result in the hand pointing towards the floor, to the use of the more powerful shoulder joint, which allows for greater power to be exerted and for the ball to travel further. The finishing position of the hand should be pointing in the intended direction of the throw. This is a key teaching point for any skill or action that involves sending any object over a distance (including kicking and hitting, which will be covered later in this chapter). Whatever the physical action performed, the finishing position of the body part being used to send that object will point in the direction the object has gone. Therefore when throwing, if pupils want the ball to go to a specific partner, their hands should end up pointing at them. The action of the arms can be mimicked by the eyes, which should follow the direction of travel.

Four key teaching points for throwing can be identified as follows:

1   The pupil stands sideways on to the target.
2   The throw comes from the shoulder.
3   The throwing hand ends up pointing at the intended target.
4   The eyes follow the direction of the ball.

Activities that can be used to develop the skill of throwing are closely linked to those that also support the development of catching skills, which we cover next. When learning throwing and catching skills it is important that pupils are given a defined working area which can be marked out by using cones (Chapter 7 explores this in further detail).

Catching

Catching involves controlling an object that has been thrown to us. This is commonly taught at the same time as the throw. It is important when catching to ensure that the object to be caught is of an appropriate size, shape and weight. When learning to catch, large, round, light balls are most effective as they give the catcher time to move to the ball as well as providing them with a larger target to catch.

It is important to have a stable body position to receive the ball. Ideally the stance should involve children standing with their feet shoulder-width apart, and with their body facing the direction from which the object is coming. As the action of the hands and arms are crucial in the development of this skill it is important that we look at these in a little more detail. Hands should form a cup shape with the little fingers together, which can be one of the most challenging parts of the skill for younger children in the earlier stages of development. There are several common reactions for pupils at this level as the ball comes towards them: to move away, to clap their hands together resulting in either the ball falling to the floor or bouncing off their hands, or to grasp the ball in a reflex gripping action similar to when a baby clutches a finger.

A child may move away from a thrown ball due to a fear of being hit, therefore we need to be conscious of the speed and direction the ball is travelling. If pupils are throwing the ball to themselves by throwing it straight up in the air, encourage them to only throw the ball up a short distance. This will also ensure that you do not have lots of balls flying around the working area. As they try to put more power into the throw pupils are likely to swing their arms too much resulting in their hands pointing over their heads thereby reducing the accuracy of their throws. If a child is throwing a ball against a wall and receiving the ball back towards their body, monitor the distance between the thrower and the wall; the closer they are the more control they will have. If a child is receiving the ball from a partner, emphasise the co-operative nature of the activity and set challenges that reward success. For example, a child scores a point only if their partner catches the ball, thereby emphasising the need for consideration in the pass being sent. When working with younger children you could consider allowing the ball to bounce before it is caught, which will reduce the speed at which it is travelling into the hands. Catching activities can be varied through using balls of different sizes and weights. A larger ball is much easier to catch due to its increased surface area. A lighter ball will travel more slowly, giving children more time to position themselves and make the catch. For those tending to catch objects using a grasping reflex, bean bags or cosh balls can be used. In all catching activities the eyes should focus on the returning object.

Four key teaching points for catching can be identified as follows:

1   The body faces the direction from which the ball is coming.
2   The hands form a cup shape, with the little fingers together.
3   As the ball comes into the hands the fingers should be cupped around the ball.
4   The caught ball should be pulled in towards the body.

The following activities can be used to develop throwing and catching skills (more activities can be found on the companion website).

Children working on their own:

1   Working in their own defined space children bounce the ball in front of themselves and attempt to catch the ball as it comes toward their waist.
2   Children throw the ball up level with their heads and catch the ball as it comes down, or alternatively allow the ball to bounce and then catch it. For added variety use different types of balls.
3   Children throw a ball against a wall and catch the ball as it rebounds (remember you can encourage them to let the ball bounce before they catch it). Once they have completed a set number of catches successfully they can be challenged to move back, increasing the distance they have to throw the ball. However, they should also be given the option of moving closer to the wall should their level of success decrease.

Children working with a partner:

1   Children can throw a ball to each other. Those who are not at a level to achieve this can start by rolling the ball to each other.
2   Over time the distance thrown can be increased. You might apply similar rules to above whereby children move further apart if successful, but move towards each other if they are not catching the ball.
3   Children can be challenged to see how many successful throws and catches they can do in a timed period.

Kicking

Kicking is used to send the ball over a distance using the feet. In some respects it can be argued that the principles associated with kicking are similar to those of the throw, with the power being generated from the hip joint (ball and socket) rather than the knee. Contact with the ball should be made with the side of the foot which has a greater surface area and will therefore provide better control than with the toe, which will tend to result in the ball being lifted into the air. When making contact, the ball should be slightly in front of the body and to the side. When sending the ball, the upper body should lean slightly over the ball with the head looking at the ball. If the head is looking up, there is a tendency for the body to lean back, which can result in the ball being lifted into the air. When kicking, the arms are used to maintain stability, remaining to the side of the body with the head looking over the ball when contact is made.

The following paired activity can be used to develop the skill.

1   Standing opposite one another, pupils pass the ball to their partner who can trap the ball by:

   a   using their hands as they would when rolling the ball to each other
   b   placing a foot on the ball to stop it
   c   moving the foot they are trapping the ball with backwards as the ball arrives (similar to the movement they will perform when catching a ball).

2   Further activities are located on the companion website.

Striking a ball

Striking the ball is an integral part of racquet sports such as tennis and badminton, and invasion games such as hockey. Objects are introduced to assist in the sending of a ball, puck or shuttlecock. We should regard these objects as extensions of our hands and as such the basic principles associated with these skills reflect many of those already discussed.

For tennis-based activities, we are introducing an extension to the hands in the form of a racquet, and in doing so we are starting to develop hand–eye co-ordination. Consequently many of the initial activities introduced will focus on the development of the ability to co-ordinate the striking of a moving object.

A good starting point is to encourage children to bounce the ball using their hands, and in doing so they will be aware of the need to co-ordinate their movements in order to carry out this activity (this is also a good starting point for teaching dribbling skills – see Chapter 7). As with the other skills discussed in this chapter, differentiation can be introduced through the types of balls used. In bouncing a ball, pupils should be encouraged to use the palm of the hand, which creates the biggest surface area, and push the ball towards the floor. They can then be encouraged to bounce a ball while simultaneously walking around their working area. This activity can be developed further by introducing a racquet these may be wooden or plastic and have varying head sizes as well as handle lengths. Having practised pushing the ball to the floor with their hands, children can repeat the activity using a racquet. You will need to emphasise that the ball should be to the front and side of the body. Pupils should be encouraged to hold the racquet as close to the racquet head as possible, especially if not using short-handled racquets, as this will allow hand–eye co-ordination to develop progressively, and pupils can slowly move their hand down the racquet shaft as they become more confident. As well as pushing the ball towards the floor, pupils can be encouraged to bounce the ball upwards, and then alternate between pushing down and bouncing upwards. This can then progress to hitting the ball towards a target; this may be a wall or a partner.

A hitting action mimics some aspects of throwing and kicking insofar as the body should be sideways on to the intended target, with the striking hand at the back and the opposite foot at the front to allow for weight transfer. The racquet should swing from back to front to meet the ball. The racquet head should finish pointing at the intended target. Again the head should follow the flight of the ball.

Once confidence in ball control has been developed and pupils are performing the skill with some efficiency, they can move on to receiving a ball from a partner. Consideration now needs to be given to the speed and direction from which the ball is fed. Normally this will be from the front, and will be performed by their partner. It is important that the feed is controlled and effective. By the time this skill is being introduced pupils should be quite proficient in throwing and catching. Initial feeds should be bounced as this will mean that the speed at which the ball is travelling is reduced. This can be achieved in the following ways.

1   Pupils feed the ball by bouncing it into a hoop, which will increase the accuracy of the feed, and then send the ball to their partner to either catch on the full, allow to bounce and then catch, or allow to roll towards them.
2   Partners feed the ball to each other using a bounce feed. Again a hoop can be used to encourage accuracy, with a downward throw being used as the feed. This ensures that the ball will then bounce up to meet the person striking the ball.

The previous section of this chapter focused on the development of fundamental motor skills. However, skill development by itself cannot provide a full appreciation of physical education. Children also need to develop an understanding of what are often referred to as motor concepts. These concepts require pupils to think about the skill they are performing in relation to their body, the space they are working in, the effort they are applying and the relationships involved. The next section of the chapter provides an overview of these, and they are discussed in greater depth in Chapter 7.

Motor concepts

The body

We have looked at the concept of the body performing movements in relation to key teaching and learning points focusing on what specific body parts do during a given skill. We have also discussed actions by the body, for example the transference of weight. We now need to consider other actions such as how the body is used to support a movement, as in performing some form of balance, and other movement concepts associated with gymnastic and dance-related activities. We can also think about the shapes the body is making, for example wide, tall, star.

Space

This concept focuses on the space in which a skill is being performed, and how this space is used within activities. In doing so we are trying to develop pupils' understanding of direction. This might be the direction they are travelling, for example forwards, backwards or sideways, the level at which they are working for example on the floor, or using pieces of equipment which will increase the height at which they are working. We should also consider the pathways children make when performing an activity, for example we can encourage them to make movement patterns on the floor either in the form of shapes (squares, circles, triangles) or letters. This latter concept was explored in Chapter 5, which looked at warming up, and also earlier in this chapter. It will be explored in further depth in Chapter 9, which looks at the promotion of cross-curricular themes.

Effort

The concept of effort is associated with the speed at which the skill is performed, for example a quick or slow movement. Do we speed up when we are performing a specific movement or do we slow down?

Relationships

The concept of relationships can include the people we are working with during a specific activity, for example alone, with a partner or with a larger group.

We have discussed specific examples in the developmental activities earlier in this chapter. We can explore the relationships we have with the objects we use, for example allowing pupils to explore different ways of moving over or under equipment. We can also think about whether we are performing the movement at the same time as someone else (sometimes referred to as unison), or after someone else thereby repeating the movement (sometimes referred to as cannon).

So far we have looked at the generic skills and concepts most relevant to pupils in the 3–8 age range. However, we should also think back to some of the previous chapters to establish whether we are covering the breadth of skills reflected in the aims of physical education (see Chapter 1) and also how these link to the overall principles of child development (see Chapter 2). As you have read this chapter you should have been keeping a record of some of the practice activities identified. Task 6.3 encourages you to develop this further.

 Task 6.4

1 For each of the fundamental motor skills, identify a series of practices you would use during your physical education lessons.
    a Where possible try these ideas in your lessons.
    b Evaluate the effectiveness of these practices noting any modifications you might make.
    c Include examples of these practices in your portfolio.

 Chapter summary

This Chapter focuses on the skills necessary to become competent in physical education activities. This is by no means an exhaustive list and further resources that may support your subject knowledge development are available on the companion website. To embed your learning from this chapter you may benefit from reflecting on the following review questions.

1 How would you define motor competence?
2 Identify a range of activities that you could use to develop pupils' ability to send and receive an object.
3 For each of the fundamental motor skills identify a series of practices you would use during your physical education lessons. Use the practices to compile a resource folder for each of the skill areas.

Further reading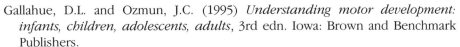

Gallahue, D.L. and Ozmun, J.C. (1995) *Understanding motor development: infants, children, adolescents, adults*, 3rd edn. Iowa: Brown and Benchmark Publishers.
This comprehensive text provides guidance on a range of fundamental movement skills and the expected stages of development.

Heath, R., Parsons, J., Stevenson, P. and Harrison, D. *Raising the bar*. Create Development.
This resource folder provides a range of activities focusing on the development of skills across the domains of learning.

PEAUK (2003) *Observing children moving*. Worcster: Tracklesport (counselling) Company.
This CD-ROM provides visual images of the development of fundamental movement skills allowing for comparisons between early and later motor patterns. It contains a wealth of resources that can be used to support learning including a detailed breakdown of each skill as well as a range of developmental activities that can be integrated into planning.

CHAPTER 7

DEVELOPING KNOWLEDGE, SKILLS AND UNDERSTANDING ACROSS AREAS OF ACTIVITY

Chapter aims

- To develop knowledge, skills and understanding across areas of activity in physical education
- To develop your depth of knowledge and understanding specific to areas of activity
- To develop practical understanding of the delivery of different areas of activity

Chapter 6 looked at the fundamental movement skills associated with the delivery of physical education. This chapter aims to build on this knowledge and understanding, with an increased focus on specific areas of activity. We will look at activities associated with athletics, dance, games, gymnastics, swimming, and OAA. Each sub-section focuses on generic principles appropriate to each area of activity, with additional practical examples located on the companion website.

Physical education has traditionally been delivered through activity areas and there has been a tendency for such activities to be focused around traditional games activities. Recently the focus has shifted towards the development of more rounded opportunities to develop a lifelong commitment to physical activity resulting in the engagement of pupils in healthy and active lifestyles beyond schooling age. There has been a move away from a purely skills-based curriculum, where success is reflected through performance, to a more learner-centred approach where learning is evident through pupils engaging in exploration and experimentation, building upon existing knowledge to construct new learning (see Chapter 2 to refresh your understanding of theories of learning and learning domains).

The next section looks in greater detail at a range of specific activities that can be taught within each area of activity. Practical activities are provided alongside discussion of how they could be delivered (supporting material is included on the companion website). A series of tasks are also included that you may wish to complete and add to your portfolio.

Athletic activities

In teaching athletics, pupils should be encouraged to engage in a range of challenges designed to develop their ability to run, throw and jump in different contexts. You will have a basic level of understanding around what key athletic events are, for example sprinting, middle distance, shot, javelin, high jump and long jump. In the primary school we are looking to introduce pupils to the concepts associated with these activities, rather than the full events themselves.

Running activities

Chapter 6 looked at running technique. Through the delivery of athletic activities, we will now look at how this technique can be developed and used in different contexts. In essence we are looking at pupils' ability to run at speed, over longer distances and over barriers.

Running for speed
Running for speed is reflected in sprint activities where the focus needs to be on shorter distances, for example 25, 50 and 100 metres. However, initially pupils should be encouraged to find out how far they can run in a specified time. Thus pupils are encouraged to work at increasing speeds through the execution of a range of challenges.

Activity   Ask pupils working in pairs to predict how far they think they will be able to run in a specified time, for example three seconds. Ask them to place a cone at the point they think they will reach in the allocated time. They are then timed by their partner and the cone is moved to the point they actually reached (this may result in the cone being moved either forwards or backwards). Pupils can then work on refining their running technique, for example working on their head position, body position, arm action and leg action, and are given the opportunity to see if they can beat their original distance. The focus is on pupils reviewing their own personal progress, rather than looking at who is the fastest.

Running for distance

Here the emphasis is on developing endurance capacity. Again the full range of activities will not need to be taught; what is important is that you look at building pupils' ability to run for extended periods of time. Again the emphasis should be placed on personal development through the setting of appropriate challenges.

Activity As with the sprinting activity identified in the previous section, cones can be used to set appropriate challenges. For example, a grid is created with cones approximately 20 metres apart. Pupils are then challenged to predict how many cones they will pass in a set time, for example three minutes. They are then timed and either count, or have their partner count the number they pass. The emphasis is on encouraging pupils to keep going over a period of time (the time can be increased based on your understanding of the group), and therefore running and walking can be used in the completion of the task. Over time the aim should be that the majority of pupils will be able to participate for the duration of the challenge. The number of cones passed should be recorded and compared with the prediction (an example recording sheet is included on the companion website). During the activity, pupils can be encouraged to think about what impact it is having on their bodies, in order that they start to develop an understanding about the impact longer periods of activity have on their bodies (see Chapter 9 for further ideas on how such activities can be used to develop cross-curricular learning).

Using skills in combination – hurdling

Activities such as hurdling can be used to combine running with other skills in order to develop pupils' abilities to co-ordinate movements. Hurdling combines running at speed with clearing an object. This might be a cane or pole which over time is increased in height. Alternatively commercially available equipment can be purchased.

Activity A good way to begin a hurdling activity is to start by asking pupils to run over a distance of 20 metres with hurdles placed at 5-metre intervals (you may wish to change the frequency of the number of hurdles). As confidence improves, the height at which the hurdles are set can be increased, for example they could be placed on cones of increasing heights, although when doing this the distance between hurdles may need to be increased. It is possible to differentiate the activity by setting up three lanes of hurdles with each lane using hurdles of a different height thereby allowing pupils to choose which lane to run in.

Jumping activities

Chapter 6 looked at the basic techniques associated with jumping for height and distance. We will now look at these in the context of athletic activities focusing specifically on the standing long jump, long jump with a walked take-off and the standing height jump.

Long jump

Activity   The standing long jump involves taking off from a static two-footed stance and jumping forward to land two-footed. The distance achieved is measured from the front of the take-off position, normally represented by a take-off board or a line on the floor, to the back of the heel of the foot landing closest to the take-off position. As with running activities, cones can be used to set targets and make predictions as to how far pupils think they will reach with their jumps. Their partners can observe their efforts and either move their cone to the point achieved or alternatively place a new cone at the landing point so the difference between the prediction and the actual jump can be identified. In the early stages, there may be a tendency for pupils to over-predict the distance they will achieve, in which case as the teacher you may wish to provide defined distances and mark these out.

As pupils start to challenge themselves further teaching points will need to be reinforced, particularly on the need to lean forward on landing in order that they do not fall back. Reciprocal cards may be used at this point which detail the specific teaching points (examples of which are available from the companion website). To encourage height in the activity, a small barrier can be placed just in front of the take-off position, which pupils need to clear before landing.

A further variation is for pupils to take a three-step walk-up, here the emphasis is on walking rather than running, and consideration will need to be given to the landing area being used. If you are fortunate enough to have access to an indoor athletics set (your feeder secondary school may have this), this should be used; alternatively you can use mats and standard health and safety concerns when using equipment apply.

Taking this activity further, pupils can start to look at combining movements, and in doing so start to perform the hop, step and jump that make up the triple jump.

Jumping for height

The standing height jump is designed to encourage pupils to think about how their bodies can be used to gain height.

Activity This activity is best taught indoors, or where a wall is available. From a standing start, pupils bend their legs and swing their arms to jump up as high as they can. As they jump they use a piece of chalk to mark the wall, or some other measure. While there are commercially available measuring devices, you may wish to provide coloured lines to identify the distances jumped. Pupils can then identify the distance achieved (for example red, amber, green), record this on their activity log and then make a second attempt. As with other examples, the activity can be performed in groups with different roles being assigned, for example performer, coach, scorer (see Chapter 3 for more information).

Throwing activities

In looking at throwing activities we are focusing on pushing (for example shot put), pulling (for example javelin) and slinging (for example discus) actions. Chapter 5 looked at the organisation and management of athletic activities and you may wish to re-read this section. The aim in throwing events is to develop pupils' competence in the activities, and in doing so it may be that you use adapted equipment. Your local secondary school may be able to source this for you.

Throwing – using a pushing action

The action of pushing an object in the context of athletic activities relates to shot put. It is likely that you will be limited in the specialist equipment to which you have access; however, equipment such as bean bags or larger balls can be used. At this level the most important point is for children to get a feel for the principles that underpin the activity.

When throwing with a pushing action the starting position sees pupils standing sideways on to the direction of throw. This will allow them over time to transfer weight and thereby increase the amount of power put into the throw. Initially this can be achieved by getting them to step into the throw; once this has been successfully accomplished they can try placing their weight on their back foot (you can even get them standing on only their back foot) before stepping forward as they throw, remembering that they must not step over the throw line.

The throwing arm is at the rear of the body (so if right-handed a pupil's left shoulder will point towards the direction of throw), with the object to be thrown held in the throwing hand and placed into the neck. Ideally the throwing arm elbow should be pointing out at right angles to the body. When ready to throw, pupils push the object forwards ideally at an angle of approximately 45 degrees. To aid the flight of the object, pupils can use their non-throwing arm to point, or alternatively pupils can identify a target on the horizon to aim at. In Chapter 6 we identified that a common principle for the flight of an object is that wherever the implement being used to send the object ends up pointing tends to reflect where the object finishes; a concept equally applicable to throwing activities.

Here is an example of how this activity can be managed within a lesson. It is equally applicable for the other types of throwing actions.

Activity   The following process can be repeated for all three types of throw. Working in groups of three, pupils assign themselves roles: a performer who completes the activity, a coach who gives feedback to the performer based on predetermined criteria (see athletics support material) and an official who has responsibility for the safety of the throw as well as the collection of the object.

The official sets up a safe throwing area, with cones used to identify throwing distances, or targeted distances, for example 5, 10 or 15 metres (it may be that in the initial stages of teaching, you as the teacher set these up). Once safety has been confirmed, the performer has three attempts at the activity. After each attempt the coach provides feedback based on the criteria sheet provided, and the official records the approximate distance (this may be related to the colour of the cone reached) and collects the thrown object. The performer then repeats the cycle until all three throws have been completed. At this point the roles are rotated so that each pupil has the opportunity to perform each role. In adopting such an approach you are limiting the number of pupils throwing and collecting at any one time, as well as introducing opportunities for developing communication and observation skills.

Throwing – using a pulling action
When throwing with a pulling action the principles involved are those associated with the javelin. Financial and health and safety concerns are likely to prevent the use of actual javelins, although foam javelins are now available which reduce many of these concerns.

The initial stance should involve pupils facing the direction of throw. If pupils seated with their legs apart this isolates the legs and arms, ensuring that the arms become the main providers of power. Pupils then hold a ball (a football or netball will suffice) behind their heads. When told to do so pupils should then release the ball forward. Typical problems that may occur in this activity include pupils releasing the ball too early so that it goes straight up in the air rather than forwards or getting insufficient height in the throw resulting in the ball making contact with their head.

A more advanced version of this activity involves pupils standing sideways on to the direction of the throw which is then made using only one hand.

Throwing – using a slinging action
In this activity the arms swing around the side of the body, and as a result this activity can potentially be the most challenging in respect of ensuring health and safety as well as the skill itself.

The key issue in this skill is the release of the object. The general principle is that the object is released from in front of the body. When thrown with the right hand, if released too early it will go to the right, if released too late it will go to the left and this has major implications for the safety of pupils to either side of the thrower. Hoops or quoits can be used for this activity. If using a hoop, the grip is with the throwing hand holding the hoop with the arm out-stretched. The arm is swung back with the hoop going towards the back of the body. Remaining outstretched, the arm is then swung around the side of the body, with the hoop being released when the arm and hand are facing forward. If a quoit is being used, then it is held with the hand over the top with the fingers gripping the far side gently.

This section has looked at the introduction and development of athletic activities including running, jumping and throwing. Included in each activity are key teaching points as well as key processes and activities to support progression. These are summarised, with further supporting materials included, on the companion website. To further consolidate your knowledge of this area you may wish to complete Task 7.1.

? Task 7.1: Athletic resources

1 Design a set of resources (one per activity) which outlines the following:

   a an overview of how the skill is performed
   b the key teaching points
   c progression activities
   d feedback opportunities.

2 Trial your resources with your class and make any modifications as you feel appropriate.
3 Add these resources to your portfolio.

Dance activities

Dance is an area of activity that is taught across the phases of the primary school. Pupils should be taught to use a range of stimuli, for example music, poetry, pictures, to co-ordinate a range of basic movement skills and concepts (see Chapter 6) in order to produce simple sequences. It provides an opportunity for pupils to gain an understanding of the different forms of dance, from different periods of time or from different cultures. This can allow them to develop an appreciation of aspects of different cultures and provides opportunities for cross-curricular teaching, an aspect explored in more detail in Chapter 9. Dance also allows for the development of communication skills associated with observation and the giving and receiving of feedback.

Activity: Animal dance This activity encourages pupils, on their own, to explore different ways of moving like animals (for example mini-beasts, jungle animals). This can be integrated into a warm-up activity.

Encourage pupils in pairs to share their ideas of animal movements with each other and to identify four moves that they can both do. At this point counting can be integrated into the performance, so that each move or series of moves has to be completed in a set time, for example by the count of 8.

They can then perform their four moves to another pair who give feedback on their performance using key words identified during the lesson introduction. These words can be displayed in the working area (the concept of word walls is developed in Chapter 9). Pupils are then provided with the opportunity to use the feedback to practise their skills again and further refine their movements.

The above activity encourages a productive approach to teaching where pupils are encouraged to explore and experiment with their own ideas and share these with others. However, you may also feel that it would be beneficial for all pupils to be doing the same moves at the same time. In dance terms this is referred to as a motif. In developing a synchronised series of movements, consideration needs to be given to the pupils' level of development.

Activity Using the animal dance developed in the previous activity you can design a motif lasting 32 beats (4 x 8 – which is the same length of time the pupils have designed their sequences to last). Pupils then practise and perform the motif, and when you are happy you can ask pupils to add their individual sequences at the end of the motif. Over time you can build this up further so that you have the format:

MOTIF – PUPIL SEQUENCE – MOTIF – PUPIL SEQUENCE – MOTIF

Another way to look at it is as a song with the motif representing the chorus!

Other potential themes can be taken from a range of teaching topics, for example the Egyptians where the stimuli for the dance could come from hieroglyphics in tombs and temples.

 Task 7.2: Dance resources

1 Design a set of resources for dance activities which outlines the following:

   a a theme/stimulus for pupils to use to develop their dance
   b key words you want pupils to use when reviewing performances.

2 Trial your resources with your class and make any modifications as you feel appropriate.
3 Add these resources to your portfolio.

Games activities

Like dance activities, games activities are taught across phases of primary education and can be used to develop pupils' abilities to perform basic skills associated with sending and receiving objects as well as moving with such objects, for example through the use of a net/wall and in striking and fielding activities and invasion activities (see Chapter 1 for more information of activity groupings). In developing competence in games-related activities, we are encouraging children to think about the correct skills to use in different situations and the strategies and tactics (for example the general principles associated with attacking and defending) required for a given activity.

Chapter 6 looked at the basic skills associated with games activities. As pupils progress there is a need to develop that range of skills further.

Dribbling

Dribbling occurs when we move with a ball, for example when running with a ball in football, hockey or basketball-based activities. It allows us to move with the ball at pace. The generic teaching points associated with the skill are that the ball should be to the side and slightly in front of the body, allowing for a greater level of control. If you have sufficient equipment, you should attempt to allow all pupils to work on their own in the first instance so that they can have the maximum opportunity to practise the skill.

Activity On their own pupils move around a defined area, identified either by the use of line markings or a coned area (see Chapter 6 for how this might be set up). If they are dribbling using their hands or their feet, they can practise using both sides of their body in an attempt to establish their preferred side. When dribbling with the hand the ball should be bounced at waist height with a pushing action. Pupils new to the skill may try to bounce the ball as high as they can, which limits precision and control. When dribbling with feet or a stick the ball needs to be kept as close to the foot or stick as possible. In the early stages of development there is a tendency for pupils to kick or hit the ball forward and then chase after it.

As pupils become more confident, they can start to speed up the skill and can be encouraged to change speed and direction (remember the principle that as the level of challenge or competition increases the quality of the skill may decrease). Chapter 5 introduced a warm-up activity whereby pupils changed speed and direction on hearing a whistle; the same activity can be used here.

Once pupils have developed a basic level of understanding and proficiency in dribbling, they can start to combine skills. They can dribble the ball over a distance and then send the ball to a partner. Initially this might be completed in small groups as follows:

1   Pupils work in groups of four.

   a   Pupils line up in pairs opposite each other.
   b   Player 1 dribbles forwards, sends the ball forward and goes to the back of the pair to whom they are running towards.
   c   Player 2 receives the ball and dribbles forward, sending the ball to Player 3.
   d   Player 3 controls the ball, dribbles forward and sends the ball to Player 4.
   e   The activity is repeated until all pupils reach their starting point.

2   Pupils work in pairs:

   a   Player 1 dribbles forward and passes the ball to Player 2.
   b   Player 1 moves into a space to receive the ball back from Player 2.
   c   The emphasis is placed on pupils looking up to see where their partner has moved to as well as thinking about the concept of space.

As with all games activities at this level the emphasis is on developing basic skills and proficiency. We are not expecting pupils to play full versions of the games but to experience small-side activities.

Net/wall activities

Chapter 6 looked at the basic principles of striking a ball. In net and wall activities, we are initially looking to develop pupils' ability to strike the ball in such a way that they can return it to their partner. Accuracy will develop over time, so that rather than sending the object to their partner, they will be able to send it into space.

We can start developing pupils' hitting skills through the use of a single personal square. As pupils progress to working with a partner they can use both squares with the middle of the squares acting as a net (see Figure 7.1).

A simple game activity can involve partners throwing the ball underarm to each other and allowing the ball to bounce prior to catching it. The emphasis is on sending the ball to the partner. Points can therefore be awarded for each successful catch. Using the same set up pupils can then use their hands as

Individual square   net

Figure 7.1   Individual square and two squares with a net in the middle

racquets to send the ball to their partner. Again the ball should bounce before it is sent back. By letting the ball bounce, the receiver has more time to get into an appropriate position before having to decide upon the speed at which the ball is travelling and where they want to send it back to. In using only the hands, the power that is generated in each hit is limited and therefore provides a safer opportunity to practise the skill.

Once pupils have progressed to an acceptable level of skill (i.e. they can control their hits so that they go to their partner), racquets can be introduced. Introducing a piece of equipment with which to hit will raise some organisational issues, for example how the racquets will be distributed (see Chapter 5 for more information on this).

Because pupils are still in the early stages of development, allocating only one racquet per pair is probably the best approach. In this way pupils can continue to use the same grid areas to carry out this activity, although hitting needs to be outwards, away from the feeder (see Figure 7.2 for a more focused explanation).

By having pupils hit outwards, the opportunities for them to hit each other are limited. However, clear guidance on the collection of balls that are not returned to partners needs to be given. For example, you need to avoid pupils running into each other's working areas, so they should wait until the ball arrives at a safe place before collecting it.

Striking and fielding activities

In striking and fielding activities we are providing opportunities for pupils to select and apply a range of existing skills (throwing, catching, striking, fielding the ball) in different contexts.

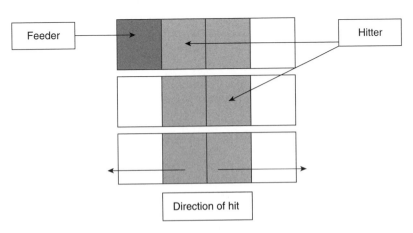

Figure 7.2 Grid areas for hitting or striking

While the principles associated with striking a ball in rounders and cricket are the same as for short tennis, the quality of the feed becomes more important. In rounders, a bowl is essentially an underarm throw, while in cricket it starts from an overarm throw position but is aimed towards the ground. One of the easiest ways of ensuring striking of the ball early on is to remove the bowler entirely. This is easily achieved through the use of cones, or tees. Doing so means that pupils are hitting the ball from a static position (as in golf) and this limits the information processing needed to co-ordinate the striking of a moving object. If we are developing striking skills associated with cricket-based activities we can use small cones (like these we might use to set out our working areas) or small tees (which are commercially available and form part of Kwik Cricket sets). For rounders activities we will need to use cones at pupil waist height, for example traffic cones (again commercial products are available).

As progress is made in the striking action, pupils can begin to receive a moving ball. Feeds can be from the side or from in front of the striker. At this point consideration needs to be given to the direction of the swing that the striking pupil will make. For example, a right-handed pupil will hit with the bat travelling from right to left, with a left-handed batter hitting from left to right. Thus the positioning of the feeder is vital to avoid injury. When progressing from a static feed (off cones) to a moving feed, the next stage is for the feed to be received from the side. When doing this the ball is dropped (you might wish to place a hoop so that the bowler can see where the ball needs to be dropped) and the striker hits the ball as it bounces back up. If you have already taught short tennis, pupils may well have experienced a similar action when bounce-feeding to themselves when starting a rally. Once pupils are confident with this the feed can come from the front, reflecting a more realistic bowling action.

As well as considering how the feed will be performed, thought needs to be given to where the struck ball will travel to. You may wish to use the practice method we introduced for net/wall activities where pupils hit outwards within their grid areas. As they progress further and group sizes increase, you might wish to adopt the fan shape introduced during throwing activities (see Chapter 5 for a more detailed explanation). This will allow you to set up more small-sided games which will enable pupils to practise their skills more.

A range of additional games activities associated with developing striking and fielding skills can be found on the companion website.

Invasion activities

Invasion activities focus on games that are associated with 'invading' an opponent's goal, such as football, rugby, netball, hockey, basketball. However, this is not an exhaustive list and more recently activities such as rock-it-ball (www. rock-it-ball.com) and pop lacrosse have started to be delivered in schools.

As with the previous activity, the use of a defined area is beneficial for management purposes. The main skills associated with such activities include throwing, catching and dribbling, although we may need to adapt the skill based on the activity being performed. As we increase the range of activities being experienced we may need to look at aspects such as trapping the ball, as in receiving a pass in football or hockey, or cradling the ball in rock-it-ball or pop lacrosse.

Once we have established the basic movement skills such as sending (throwing, kicking), receiving (catching, trapping) and moving with the ball (dribbling) we can start to think about basic games-related skills, for example the use of space, shooting, basic games play.

Throughout, the emphasis should be placed on playing small-sided games (for example 3 v 3) which allow for maximum participation and give pupils more opportunities to practise skills. Again the use of defined areas allows for greater levels of management, for example if the pupils are playing a 2 v 2 game, then they can use four squares, a 3 v 3 game would then use six grids (Figure 7.3).

The use of coned areas allows you to control the movement of pupils in the early stages of development by confining their movements to either their own area or across two adjacent areas (a principle evident in netball). Alternatively they can be used to create 'safe areas' where the number of pupils allowed in is restricted, which offers some protection for pupils with less confidence.

Common skills that we can develop include moving into a space to receive the ball, basic interception skills and skills associated with scoring points.

Earlier in this chapter we identified basic relay activities where pupils worked in small groups to pass and follow the ball. In more realistic games activities, pupils are more likely to pass the ball and then move into a space.

Activity In pairs pupils pass the ball to each other. Once they have passed they move into a new space to receive the ball. The next progression is for the

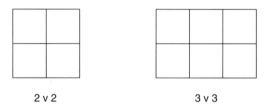

2 v 2   3 v 3

Figure 7.3 Grids for a 2 v 2 and 3 v 3 game

same 'game' to be played in groups of four (the easiest way to get to this number is to ask two pairs to join together). At this point, rather than sending the ball back to the person who sent it, an opportunity for decision making occurs, whereby the receiver has to think about who the best person to send the ball to is.

Once pupils have become confident and competent, you can start to introduce a defender into the activity. This is a progression for groups of both three and four, and in essence reflects the playground game of 'piggy in the middle'. Within this practice all pupils become involved in more complex decision-making opportunities. The sender has to think about who is best placed to receive the ball based on the position of their team mates and also the position of the defender. The receivers need to think about where they are best placed in relation to their team mates and the defender. The defender has to decide who to mark. If working in groups of four the attacking team (three people) have more time to make a decision so, if the learning objectives of the activity are based around attacking, this is a better group size than working in groups of three where the balance between attack and defence is more evenly distributed. To score a point the attacking team has to complete a set number of passes without the ball being touched or intercepted (this figure is flexible and should be based on the ability of the pupils). Once the point has been scored or the ball touched or intercepted, the defender becomes an attacker and vice versa. Before moving on, all pupils should have experienced both attacking and defending roles.

The activity can be developed further by bringing together two groups (3 v 3 or 4 v 4). The previous activity can then be repeated, although you may set a higher number of passes that need to be completed before a point is scored (this can be different for each team). Alternatively scoring areas can be introduced. These might be in the form of end zones (as you would find in American football), where a goal is scored if the ball is received in the end zone, or actual goals, for example the ball must be bounced in a hoop, or passed through a set of cones.

One issue that can occur with these activities is a tendency for pupils to start following the ball. If this is occurring you may consider restricting the areas as mentioned earlier in the chapter, so, for example, a maximum of two pupils are allowed in any one area (see Figure 7.4).

Consideration should also be given to the location of the goal. If the goal is located in the middle of the end zone, typically the pattern of play will be up and down the middle of the playing area. If you want to increase the use of the playing area and also the movement of the play across it, you can consider setting up two goal areas at each side of the end zone. A further adaptation is to set scoring areas along the side of the playing zone (in this case it is best to use coloured goals so that each team is clear about which colour they need to score in). As with all the activities included in this chapter, supporting work cards and information are included on the companion website.

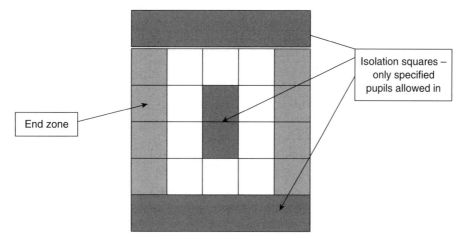

Figure 7.4 Grid showing restricted areas

As pupils' competence levels develop, more easily recognisable versions of games can start to be played. For example, Kwik Cricket is a modified version of cricket but played in groups of up to 12, with teams made up of pairs for scoring purposes. High 5 Netball is played with teams of five players offering more space and time for decision making to occur. Further information on these can be found on the companion website.

It is important that, as pupils' skills, knowledge and understanding increase, opportunities are created that allow them to develop within the affective domain through working effectively in groups to create, participate in and manage games activities. In doing so they can begin to take responsibility for game creation (see Chapter 3 for more information on Teaching Games for Understanding and Sport Education), as well as refereeing and umpiring games activities.

 Task 7.3: Games activities resources

1 Design a set of resources for one net/wall, one striking and fielding, and one invasion activity (one per activity) which outlines the following:

a a range of skills per area
b a series of games activities.

2 Trial your resources with your class and make any modifications as you feel appropriate.
3 Add these resources to your portfolio.

Gymnastic activities

Gymnastic activities build upon the fundamental movement skills associated with locomotion and stability (see Chapter 6). Pupils should be given opportunities to develop these skills working on their own and in groups and to perform skills on different equipment. As with dance activities, gymnastic movements can be linked together to produce sequences which pupils can perform and receive feedback on.

In breaking down the requirements for gymnastic activities further we can focus on skills associated with travelling, jumping and balance.

Travelling

In travelling, we are looking at pupils' ability to move between two points. This might be in the form of rotation, which might include simple rolls such as a log roll (also referred to as a pencil roll), an egg roll, a side roll, or a circle roll (also referred to as a teddy bear roll), or more developmentally challenging rolls such as forward and backward rolls. Further information on the specific teaching points for each of these rolls can be found on the companion website.

However, travelling can take many other forms. For example, you can ask pupils to explore different ways of travelling using different body parts, or to copy how different animals might move (an idea we have already explored in the section on dance activities).

Activity   As a warm-up activity, pupils move around a designated area using different body parts, such as hands and feet, side, bottom, front (these should be identified by the class teacher to ensure appropriate health and safety regulations are enforced). Alternatively pupils could copy different ways in which animals move, for example if the pupils are exploring a topic in class around mini-beasts, they could imitate the movements of different creatures such as a ladybird, butterfly, caterpillar or snail.

During the warm up, pupils can explore a range of different ways of travelling. They can practise these on the floor to improve performance. At this point key words may be introduced, which can be posted on the walls of the gym or hall in the form of a word wall. Pictorial display cards can also be used to support those who struggle with ideas.

Pupils can share the different movements they have identified with a partner, choosing three movements that they can both perform (this process can also be used for rolling activities as well as forming the basis for the introduction and development of other skills around jumping and balance). They should then practise these to improve their performances. Pupils can note their movements down using a gymnastics storyboard (see the companion website for examples) to produce a record of their developing sequence.

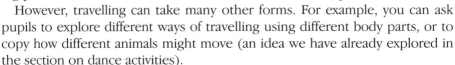

Once pupils have become competent in performing travelling movements on the floor, they can be introduced to small apparatus, for example benches, movement tables, and can transfer their sequence onto this equipment.

Developing this activity further, each pair can join up with another group to perform their sequence. They should start by describing their sequence to the other pair using the storyboard to support them. They can then perform their sequence to each other, receiving feedback about their performance from the observing pair. Feedback should be focused around the key words you have introduced at the start of the lesson, and again you might find it useful to use focused word walls. Pupils should then have the opportunity to go away and practise their sequence based on the feedback they have received.

Jumping

Chapter 6 looked in some detail at different types of jump, so you may wish to refer back to this now. You can adopt a similar progressive approach to the previous activity by asking pupils to explore different ways of jumping. They then share their ideas with a partner, identifying a series of jumps that they can both perform. Individual feedback is provided using key words held on the word wall. Their jumps are then added to their original travelling storyboard. You may wish to give a set of skill pictures to each group which will not only provide them with examples of the movements they can perform, but also allow them to stick these onto their story boards to aid feedback and recall skills. (An example set is provided on the companion website.)

If appropriate, pupils can be encouraged to perform jumping activities using equipment. They will need to be taught about safe practice associated with jumping onto, over and off equipment (see Chapter 5). They can also start to think about the shapes they make when jumping allowing for the introduction of specific jumps such as straight, tuck and straddle.

Balancing

Balancing is usually associated with being still. As with the section looking at travelling, during the lesson warm up, we can provide pupils with the opportunity to explore balances using different body parts. These body parts may be referred to as large (or patches), for example shoulders, side, bottom, or small (or points), for example hands, feet, elbows, knees. You can introduce the different body parts or provide pictorial resource cards to support those who struggle to come up with ideas.

The model applied in the previous activities can also be used here, with pupils exploring ideas on their own, sharing these with a partner and then adding them to their emerging sequence. By the end pupils should have a storyboard containing travel, jump and balance movements.

As the sequence evolves, pupils can start to think about how they can perform it using apparatus. Pupils will need to consider the key concepts introduced in Chapter 6 associated with direction, level and speed. They can start to build upon their prior learning focusing specifically on improving their effectiveness in executing a skill as well as looking at a wider range of apparatus that can be used.

 Task 7.4: Gymnastic resources

1 Design a set of resource cards for a range of rolling, jumping and balancing skills which outlines the following:

   a key teaching points for each skill
   b a series of progression activities for pupils to complete
   c key words pupils need to use when giving feedback.

2 Trial your resources with your class and make any modifications as you feel appropriate.
3 Add these resources to your portfolio.

Swimming activities and water safety

When teaching swimming activities to pupils, emphasis should be placed on the development of water confidence and safety, including entry into and exit out of the water, as well as what happens when pupils are in it. Pupils should then be provided with opportunities to learn a range of swimming strokes in order that they can swim the recommended distance of 25 metres (DfEE, 1999). Chapter 6 introduced the concept of FUNdamentals (British Gymnastics). In the context of swimming activities our initial teaching needs to focus on balance, agility and co-ordination, progressing to gliding, speed, sculling and floating.

Developing water confidence

To develop water confidence, emphasis needs to be placed on getting pupils familiar with the water, including entry and exit. In looking at how pupils should enter and exit the pool, consideration needs to be given to the depth of the pool, whether steps are available and special needs of pupils (Chapter 5 provides further information on health and safety issues associated with using swimming pools).

Once pupils are confident entering and exiting the pool, consideration can be given to developing their confidence in the water. Basic warm-up activities similar to those identified in the earlier sections looking at dance and gymnastics can be used in order to get pupils to explore different ways of travelling through water. 'Toys' can be used to introduce an element of play through games activities, for example floating objects and sinking objects. Pupils can be encouraged to blow objects across the pool, drop objects into the water and then go underwater to retrieve them, and throw and catch objects in the water. Alternatively you can call out different actions or shapes you want pupils to make, for example jump up, bob down, make a star (which could be floating face up, floating face down, standing up). Simple activities such as 'washing their face' or 'ring a ring o' 'roses' can also be used to encourage pupils to submerge themselves.

As always, organisation of the working space is important. In the teaching of physical education lane ropes can be used to section off work areas. These might be lengthways, but can also be attached across the width of the pool.

Once pupils are confident in the water you can start to look at more specific skill development. In terms of stroke development we can identify common principles, specifically body position, leg action, arm action, breathing and co-ordination (which relates specifically to breathing).

Body position

Here we are focusing on pupils' ability to hold a floating position, which may be on their back or their front. The focus is on the creation of a streamlined position. In many respects this position is similar to the starting position for a log roll/straight roll or the position in flight achieved when doing a straight jump. In linking it to other skills which they may have already performed, pupils can start to think about how they can apply skills across different contexts.

Once pupils are able to perform this position they should be encouraged to push and glide. This involves pushing from the side of the pool and forming an arrow shape to see how far they can travel (see the companion website for a more detailed analysis). Common faults which may occur include the feet sinking resulting in the body bending from the middle. This can be rectified by encouraging pupils to tense their stomach muscles, or through the use of a floatation belt.

Leg action

Once pupils become confident at pushing and gliding from the side of the pool, we can start looking at the leg action of the stroke being taught. For many the first stroke they learn will be breast stroke. This is mainly due to the fact that the stroke can be performed without the head going under water so breathing is easier.

Initial activities can encourage pupils to practise the skill from a static position. This might include holding on to the side with their hands and then performing the skill. This approach allows you to observe the kick itself. Where pupils struggle to keep their feet up, floatation belts can again be used. As progress is made pupils can be asked to push away from the side and, using a handheld float, perform the leg action to travel across the pool. If pupils have the confidence to submerge their faces, they should be encouraged to do this, coming up for air as appropriate. This will encourage the streamline position.

Arm action

The next step is to introduce the arm action. There is a need here to isolate the arms, so any floatation aids are now used by the legs. Again depending upon the stroke being taught, variation in arm action will be evident. When practising breast stroke the hands push forward to straighten the arms. With palms facing outwards a semi-circle is drawn by each hand with the finishing point in line with the chest, before hands push forward once again.

Breathing

Once the arm movement has been introduced, activities aimed at combining both the leg and arm action can be developed. At this point the focus should be on breathing. Breathing in beginner breast stroke swimmers is a slow exhalation of breath followed by a deep breath inwards. Because the head tends to be above the water level this is easier than for other strokes. As they become more proficient and the hands move forward the head will bob down and the swimmer will breathe out underwater, with the intake of breath occurring as the hands make their semi-circular movements which will naturally cause the head to rise slightly. Further analysis of the other strokes can be found on the companion website.

 Task 7.5: Swimming activities resources

1 Design a set of resources for each stroke which outlines the following:

   a how the skills should be performed (pictures)
   b the key teaching points for each aspect of the stroke
   c differentiated activities for beginners, intermediate swimmers and advanced swimmers.

2 Trial your resources with your class and make any modifications as you feel appropriate.
3 Add these resources to your portfolio.

Outdoor adventurous activities

While not commonly taught in primary schools, OAA offers pupils opportunities to participate in a range of challenges across different learning environments. Skills associated with problem solving and basic orienteering can be developed, as can social skills associated with working in groups and in challenging situations. In some respects it is the contribution to the development of skills within the affective domain (see Chapter 2) that marks OAA out from other aspects of the physical education curriculum. There is also a general lack of confidence among primary school teachers in the delivery of the activities, which for many are seen as dangerous, or as carrying a higher than acceptable level of risk. You will need specialist qualifications to deliver those more 'risky' activities and for many of you your pupils will experience to them during a residential experience. However, simple problem-solving and orienteering activities can be delivered by most people.

Problem solving

Problem-solving activities provide opportunities for pupils to develop knowledge, skills and understanding of working in group situations as pupils are required to engage in a range of different roles and responsibilities. While specific motor skills may not be developed, it is the associated development both within the cognitive and affective domains of learning that encourages pupils to transfer existing knowledge, skills and understanding and apply them to different situations.

Activity: Shepherd and sheep   In this activity the emphasis is placed on effective communication using a variety of methods. Working in pairs, one pupil is blindfolded. Their partner is then responsible for guiding them along a path (which can be set out using cones) avoiding obstacles that may have been placed along the path. The guide may choose to hold their partner's hand or describe the obstacles as they approach. As pupils become more confident they can call out instructions from a distance, for example forwards, backwards, step over, bend down. The final progression is for two pairs to join together. One pupil becomes the shepherd, who has responsibility for communicating to the other pupils (the sheep). They can be encouraged to use other forms of communication, for example whistles to direct the sheep into a pen.

At the end of the activity, pupils can feedback to each other about what they felt went well and how they might improve next time. In doing so they are developing skills associated with communicating with others through the giving and receiving of feedback. What is important at this point is that pupils have the opportunity to use the feedback they receive to make improvements to their approach.

Activity: Group spell   In this activity, pupils are required to work in small groups to spell as many words as they can using their bodies to form the letters. Points can be awarded relative to the number of letters contained within the word (for example a three letter word would be awarded three points). Time limits can be set so pupils have to make as many words as they can in two minutes.

Activity: Bench swap   This activity requires pupils to change positions while standing on a bench. If they fall off the bench they must return to the spot on the bench they started at. Having randomly stood on the bench, you ask pupils to change positions so that they become ranked, for example in height order with the shortest pupil at the front and the tallest at the back. Using balancing and supporting techniques pupils swap places with each other until this is achieved. Once they have achieved their ranking you can ask them to swap again so they are ranged by, for example, month of birth, day of birth, shoe size.

These are just a few ideas that you can use. Further examples can be found on the companion website.

Orienteering

Orienteering-focused activities can be as simple as following trails to encouraging pupils to develop those skills associated with map reading.

Trails

Pupils can be asked to follow simple trails set out in the school grounds, for example they could follow a string that is laid out to form a course. Once they become confident with the activity they can be blindfolded with a partner giving them instructions. Map reading and drawing skills can be developed with pupils drawing simple plans and maps, or through the use of more detailed maps.

Activity: Designing and using simple maps   The basic concepts of a map will need to be explained to pupils at the outset, for example that it is a two-dimensional representation of an area. Working in pairs pupils draw a simple plan of the gym or outdoor space where the lesson is taking place. Using a key or legend they should include features such as windows, doors, wall bars, benches, mats (if indoors) or pitch markings, playground markings, trees, benches (if working outdoors).

The next step is for pupils to design a course for someone to follow using their map. In orienteering a course is completed by collecting a stamp from locations identified on a map. These stamps are attached to controls which are red and white in colour. While these can be bought for use in schools (orien-teering equipment packs are commercially available) a simple red and white card can be made and laminated with letters or numbers written on them. Plastic cups can also be used with coloured pencils attached to identify which control has been visited. Permanent courses can be established within the school grounds by painting numbers and letters on permanent fixtures, for example walls and fences (make sure you get permission to do this from the school). Further details on setting up orienteering courses and resources can be found on the companion website.

Using their maps pupils can be asked to design a course by putting red cir-cles on the map where they have placed their controls. Each control should be numbered, but this does not mean that they have to be collected in that order. On a separate piece of paper they can record the control number and whatever piece of information is on the card. For example, if the course requires pupils to collect a series of letters which can be used to spell a word, then the record card would show the control number and corresponding let-ter. Once the course has been set up, pupils swap maps and complete each other's courses.

Developing this idea further, you can produce a map of the school grounds (this can be done commercially, or simply by acquiring a copy of the school plan). You can then identify a series of courses which can be differentiated by the distance pupils have to cover and the difficulty of finding the controls. Alternatively you can set up timed events where pupils have a set time to find as many controls as they can. Different controls will carry different points so those that are close to the starting point and easy to find are worth fewer points than those that are further away or are harder to find. In this way pupils are engaging in planning activities prior to the task to think about strategies they might employ to get the most points.

As with any aspect of learning, activities need to be structured in such a way that pupils become confident in the process they are engaging in. Chapter 2 talked about scaffolding of learning, and it is likely that pupils will find this approach helpful when first introduced to the concept of orienteering. In prac-tice this could be achieved by walking through a course so pupils know what they are looking for. As they become confident you may wish to let some of them continue with the course on their own while you walk the rest of the class round the course. Alternatively pupils can engage in a 'star event' which requires them to return to the start point after visiting each control so that you can check on their progress and give feedback.

You can also be creative in what pupils have to do at each control. For exam-ple, each control could have an assigned letter and these letters could either form a word or be used to make as many words as possible. A similar approach can be used with numbers and mathematical symbols so that they solve a prob-lem. Alternatively pupils could complete the course in groups and at each control have a problem to solve.

Reviewing activities

Reviewing activities can be used extensively within OAA as a means of getting pupils to reflect upon their own performance and the performances of others. In their simplest form they can be used by pupils to identify what went well (WWW) with the activity, or 'even better if' (EBI) to identify the improvements they would wish to make. Alternatively they can be used to support pupils' reflections upon their feelings during each activity. Using chuff charts pupils can rate their 'chuffness' at specific time points during the activity. This approach is particularly useful for reflecting on longer events when you have taken pupils on a residential experience.

Task 7.6: OAA resources

1 Design a set of resources for problem-solving activities (one per activity) which outlines the following:

   a a problem-solving task (to include the equipment you will need)
   b key points that might help pupils to solve the problem
   c review activities which encourage pupils to reflect upon how they achieved the activity.

2 Trial your resources with your class and make any modifications as you feel appropriate.
3 Add these resources to your portfolio.

Chapter summary

This chapter has attempted to provide a general overview of a range of activities that can be taught in the primary school. However, this is not an exhaustive list and further resources are available from the companion website. As you have read the chapter you will have identified commonalities in how activities can be taught. Perhaps the three most important points are as follows.

1 Wherever possible progress pupils from working on their own, to working with a partner, to working in small groups.
2 Give pupils opportunities for exploration and experimentation rather than just telling them how to perform a skill. This will allow them to modify the skill to their individual needs.
3 Practices are transferable across activities.

The following review questions give you the opportunity to review your learning through this chapter.

1 What are the key skills that need to be developed within each area of activity?
2 How can teaching in physical education support learning across the domains of learning?
3 What approaches to teaching are applicable across the areas of activity?

Further reading

Griggs, G. (2007) *Physical education: the essential toolkit for primary teachers.* Blackburn: Educational Printing Services Limited.
This guide to the teaching of physical education offers a range of practical examples for including within your lessons.

Hall, J. (2004) *Primary physical education handbook*. London: A & C Black.
This provides another range of practical examples for teaching primary physical education as well as supporting materials for the delivering of the subject as a whole.

Price, L. (2003) *Primary school gymnastics: teaching movement action successfully*. London: David Fulton Publishers.

UK Athletics Ltd (2005) Elevating athletics.
This resource published by UK Athletics (academy.uka.org.uk/elevating-athletics) provides comprehensive guidance regarding the delivery of athletic activities. Guidance is also provided on inclusion and planning.

CHAPTER 8

PLANNING THE LEARNING EXPERIENCE

Chapter aims

- To develop an understanding of the processes involved in developing effective learning experiences
- To develop an understanding of the process of planning and its application within physical education
- To develop an understanding of assessment and its effective use within teaching and learning
- To integrate existing knowledge within the process of planning

Previous chapters have focused on developing your knowledge and understanding of the constituent parts of physical education. This chapter aims to draw these together to provide you with the opportunity to look at how they can be used in the planning of learning experiences, as well as how continuity and progression in the learning experiences of pupils can be achieved. If you have not looked at some of these chapters for a while, it might be worth re-reading them (or completing the summary questions at the end of each chapter) to allow you to refresh your understanding.

A good starting point is to think about why we need to plan, as it is important that we have an understanding of why it is necessary if we are to accept it as an essential process and thereby give it the importance that it needs.

Task 8.1

1 On your own reflect on what planning means to you.
2 Think about situations in which you have used some form of planning.

   a What were the advantages of planning?
   b Did you experience any problems when planning?

3 Now share these with a partner.

   a What similarities and differences did you find?

4 From these conversations:

   a identify three key benefits of planning.
   b identify three key factors you think you should take into account when planning.

You have had an opportunity to reflect on what planning means to you; we now delve a little deeper. Effective planning requires us to look at the whole picture of what we want to achieve. Planning can be short term, what we want to achieve in a lesson (a lesson plan); medium term, where we are looking at what we want to achieve over a period, for example a term (scheme of work); and long term, what we might want to achieve over a year, or a key stage (National Curriculum).

QCDA (2010a: 24–25) identifies three key questions that we should look to address when engaging in any planning process, broken down into a seven-step design and planning process. While individual schools may adopt different approaches the principles involved in the process will be similar.

Focus within the seven-step process is centred on three key themes.

- What are you trying to achieve?

  o Identify your priorities.
  o Record your starting point.
  o Set clear goals.

- How will you organise learning?

  o Design and implement a lesson.

- How will you know you are achieving your aims?

  o Review progress.
  o Evaluate and record the impact.
  o Maintain, change or move on.

We will now explore these in more detail.

What are you trying to achieve?

When working with student teachers around the planning process I encourage them to think about the end of the lesson as their starting point. In particular I ask them to picture what it will look like, focusing specifically on what the pupils will be doing. I then get them to think about what they will need to include within the lesson to ensure the picture is achieved. By doing this you can start to plan the activities you wish to include within the lesson as well as thinking about how you will move between these activities. The initial plan may be in the form of a 'mind map' or as bullet points, which you develop further when you engage in the formal planning process. In planning you are thinking not only about the pupils with whom you are working, but also about yourself. Knowing what you are doing and when provides an element of security for you. It gives you a sense of purpose and direction as well as allowing you time to prepare and organise resources.

Looking at what the focus of the lesson is to be allows us to reflect on our own priorities, and clearly identify what we want our learners to achieve. It allows us to think about the order in which activities might be placed to provide continuity, ensuring that activities build upon what has already been taught. It also provides us with the opportunity to think about what information or knowledge we will need to complete subsequent tasks. When looking to promote continuity we are focusing on delivering the curriculum. However, we also need to ensure that there is some form of progression in the activities taught. Progression focuses on knowledge acquisition and application, ensuring that pupils are challenged at an appropriate level.

From such explanations you can start to see how both terms, continuity and progression, are closely aligned; in fact they tend to be referred to together. Such terminology and principles should not be new to you as they are linked to the theories associated with learning (see Chapter 2). They also link to the ideas explored in Chapter 4, where we looked at inclusion and differentiation in more depth.

As we start to look at planning in greater depth, we need to consider the make up of the class we are working with. This links to our starting point. What experiences have the pupils already had? How will you build on what they already know and understand? For example: What were they taught last year? What have they been taught in other subject areas? You may also need to think about the make up of the group, for example their age, number and gender. This will be particularly relevant if the group you are teaching is different from your base class.

You will need to consider what you want to achieve by the end of the scheme as well as how many lessons you have in which to accomplish this. These basic questions will form part of any planning meetings you may be involved in. They are also some of the questions you may be expected to ask during orientation visits for school placement.

Our final consideration in this section is to look at the goals or learning objectives we wish pupils to achieve. Shilvock and Pope summarise the process as follows:

> before planning a lesson it is important to identify your exact learning objectives. Consider your students' learning as a long journey. Before setting off you need to be clear where you are, decide where you want to go and the most effective route for getting there. By outlining your objectives at the start of the lesson, students will have a clear idea of where they are heading and why and can be informed of progress along the way to make the journey more fulfilling. Students will follow your instructions in lesson and do what you ask, but won't know the purpose of separate activities unless you explain. (2008: 35)

So we have identified our journey's end and considered our starting point. It is now time to look at writing our objectives. Learning objectives provide the initial structure for the lesson – you might say that they are the skeleton of the lesson. As such they need to reflect what you want pupils to achieve by the end of the lesson. Again there is no one-size-fits-all approach to the process. Davison and Leask identify learning objectives as 'specific statements which set out what pupils are expected to learn from a particular lesson in a way that allows you to identify if learning has occurred' (2005: 81). What is important here is the phrase 'allows you to identify if learning has occurred'; your learning objectives not only outline what you are striving to achieve within the lesson, they also provide you with terms of reference against which you can assess the learning that has taken place, as well as a framework against which you can evaluate your overall lesson. They allow you to provide clarity of instructions to the pupils in your class by being specific about what you are expecting. A number of schools use the anagrams WALT (We Are Learning To …) and WILF (What I'm Looking For ….). When first starting to work in a school it is important that you identify the approaches adopted.

In the context of physical education we are looking predominantly at what we want pupils to know, perform and apply and at how they evaluate their own and other performances. It is important that you are clear about what you want them to do, in what situation and what it will look like, which draws on both WALT and WILF. Thus a learning objective for gymnastics might be: to be able to perform three balances (what you want them to do) in a sequence (in what situation) demonstrating good body tension through pointed toes and being still (what it will look like). The companion website provides further examples of learning objectives.

However, if we are to reflect the diverse nature of the classes we teach we need to consider if we can only use one learning objective. While the example provided is generic in its writing as it does not specify the types of balance or the length of sequence, you might wish to consider writing learning objectives that link to different levels of attainment. Some schools use 'All pupils will …', 'Most pupils will …' and 'Some pupils will …'. Using such sentence beginnings allows you to identify what you want everyone to be able to do, what you are expecting most pupils to be able to do, and what you acknowledge only some of the pupils will be able to achieve. This also allows you to identify key performance indicators which can be linked to formal assessment activities.

Regardless of the approach you adopt, it is important, as Shilvock and Pope (2008) identify, that you share these learning objectives with pupils at the start of the lesson in order that they have a clear understanding of the lesson 'journey'. Of equal importance is the need for pupils to refocus on these objectives in order that they can assess where they are and what they need to do next in order to achieve the objective. Consequently the depth and complicity of the objectives you set or share with pupils will vary across age groups. What is important is that your learning objectives are not something that you keep to yourself. They should be shared with the pupils, for example written on a board and explained at the start of the lesson, as well as referred back to throughout the lesson.

The quality of your objectives will directly impact on your ability to evaluate both the performance of the pupils and how the lesson was taught. Time spent in this initial process is therefore important. Task 8.2 provides you with an opportunity to put some of this into practice.

 Task 8.2: Setting learning objectives

The previous section looked at the initial phase of lesson planning, focusing predominantly on the identification of learning goals and objectives.

Using the case study below and working either on your own or in a small group, identify three learning objectives for the lesson (the companion website provides you with some working examples).

 Case study

You are to teach your Year 2 class of 32 basic ball-handling skills. The class is made up of 15 boys and 17 girls. In Year 1 they were introduced to throwing and catching using large soft balls. By the end of the scheme of work, only eight pupils could consistently catch the ball when thrown to them, with the rest of the class able to catch the ball if it was bounced. Very few of the class could throw, and those who could lacked direction and distance, tending to throw the ball from a forward facing position.

The start of this chapter identified three main focal points within planning, the second of which focuses around the organisation of the learning. The next section of the chapter therefore looks at the design and implementation of the lesson, and builds on aspects covered in Chapters 3, 4, 6 and 7.

How will you organise learning

When designing and implementing a lesson there are a number of aspects that need to be considered. While the objectives might be the skeleton of the lesson, the design and content form the flesh. In this section we will start to consider aspects of lesson design focusing specifically on:

- what we want pupils to do
- how we plan to organise pupils
- how we will ensure that all pupils are able to achieve
- the specific material that we will need to cover, and at which point in the lesson.

This section clearly identifies what the lesson will look like. If the objectives are a 'journey' this section is 'a recipe'.

As mentioned previously in this chapter, different organisations will plan in different ways and use different templates on which to plan. Below is an example of a planning template (Figure 1) that you might fine useful (it is likely that your training establishment or school will provide additional examples of planning templates).

If we now start to think about how we will use this template, we first need to identify our learning objectives. If you have already completed Task 8.2 you can use those as your learning objectives, although a working example is provided below.

Learning objectives:

- To be able to send and receive the ball over different distances showing accuracy
- To develop the ability to play small-sided games
- To be able to review your own performance and identify ways of improving.

If we unpick these learning objectives, we are looking at developing pupils' abilities to send and receive a ball (this could be throwing and catching, kicking and trapping, hitting and field) over different distances. We want them to be able to demonstrate these skills within small-sided games and demonstrate accuracy in their passing. We also want them to review their own performance. Therefore we need to ensure that within the lesson opportunities arise for pupils to practise sending and receiving, and that this occurs over varying distances. They need to develop an understanding of what a successful pass looks like, so we need to ensure that at some point we give them clear terms of reference (learning or teaching points) that give them a framework against which they can assess their own performance and that of others. Finally, we need to include opportunities for them to demonstrate their skill development within a small-game situation. This is the basis of our lesson, and would

Class		Number of pupils	Gender	
Lesson number		Lesson length		

Previous experience

Evaluation from previous lesson (focus should be on pupil learning)

Lesson objectives

Equipment needed

Lesson content

Timing	Activity	Organisation	Equipment	Differentiation (space, task, equipment, people)

Figure 8.1   Planning template

be reflected in our planning template within the lesson objectives section (see Figure 8.2).

As with any lesson we need to look at the constituent parts, be it a three-, four- or five-part lesson. When using a three-part lesson structure you will need to plan a starter activity, move on to main activities (which may include skills practices as

Class		Number of pupils	Gender	
Lesson number		Lesson length		

Previous experience

Evaluation from previous lesson

Lesson objectives

- To be able to send and receive the ball over different distances showing accuracy
- To develop the ability to play small-sided games
- To be able to review your own performance and identify ways of improving

Equipment needed

Lesson content

Timing	Activity	Organisation	Equipment	Differentiation (space, task, equipment, people)
	Starter			
	Main activities			
	Plenary			

Figure 8.2 Planning template including lesson objectives

well as games-based activities) and then ensure enough time is available to bring the lesson to a conclusion through a plenary. Opportunities for pupils to engage in evaluative processes should be integrated throughout the lesson. Once you have an image of the lesson you can start to look at each part of the lesson in more depth.

When planning many people focus on the taught part of the lesson, rather than the lesson in its entirety. Traditionally in physical education the starter activity would be seen as a warm up (see Chapter 5 for the purpose and components of a warm up). However, your lesson starts from the time pupils begin to change and therefore this should be included in your planning. Are there any set routines you expect pupils to follow while changing? How will you supervise changing? What will pupils do when they are changed? Is there anything you can get them to do once they have changed, for example find a partner and talk about what they can remember from the last lesson?

Consideration also needs to be given to the general organisation of the lesson. Effective organisation limits the time pupils spend off task (that is the time when learning is not taking place).

Key questions to consider here are as follows.

- How will I group my pupils?

  o Do I want pupils to be of similar ability or do I want to mix them up?
  o What group size do I need?
  o What is the optimum size for the activity – can the activity be done alone? One point to think about is that the smaller the group, the more opportunities occur for pupils to engage in the activity.
  o How can I get them into groups?

If you refer back to Chapter 4 we introduced the concept of groupings.

- Will I need to change the group sizes through the lesson?

  o How can I minimise group size changes?
  o What is the final group size (threes, fours)?
  o How will I get there?

For example, if you have planned for the end game to be played as 4 v 4 you might have pupils working on their own to begin with, then with a partner, and then get two pairs to join to form a group of four. The key is to avoid splitting groups once they have been formed, for example going from pairs to threes.

- What equipment do I need and where will this be placed?

  o How will equipment be collected and returned to the store?

Are you going to have full responsibility for taking the equipment out and bringing it back, or is this a task you can give to designated pupils? A key point to note is that it is your responsibility to ensure that all equipment is fit for purpose (see Chapter 5) and also that all equipment taken out is returned. You need to train your pupils to count the equipment out as well as counting it back in. It is also important that equipment stores are kept tidy, not only because it means that your equipment will last longer, but also because you will not waste time trying to find equipment at the start of the lesson.

o How will pupils collect equipment for each activity?

This might seem like an odd question, but I am sure that you can all remember racing to choose the brightest ball, and everyone fighting over the new equipment – at times choosing your equipment became a survival of the fitest, or whoever got their first. If you have pupils working on their own, identify a small group at a time to go and collect their equipment or hand the equipment out as you are talking to them. If they are working in pairs or small groups, get them to identify an individual with responsibility to collect the equipment. You may set up equipment stations so that pupils go to different places to collect what they need. It is important to consider when the best time to collect the equipment is. You will want to avoid handing out and collecting in equipment too frequently. You also need to consider what pupils do with their equipment when you are explaining the next activity, for example do they leave it where they are working or do they bring it with them, which risks them playing with it while you are trying to talk.

- What space do I have and how can I make effective use of it?

  o How will I designate boundaries?

Traditionally physical education lessons will take place in the school hall, or on the school playground or field. If you are teaching inside, you will need to be very conscious of other equipment that might be stored in that area, for example lunch tables, chairs, pianos. Thinking back to Chapter 5, you need to ensure that the area is safe for use. You may consider using cones to form your boundary areas. However, you will also need to think about the progressions in your lessons and how you may need to change the space over time.

If you are outside, you may need to consider other users.

  o Does your lesson take place when another class is having their break?
  o What line markings do you have available?
  o Can you have line markings added?

Over recent years there has been an increase in the use of the playground and development of playground markings and 'playzones'. Again the facilities you have will vary between schools, so you should spend time familiarising yourself with what you have available prior to undertaking any detailed planning.

In terms of organisation we need to be clear about what behaviour management strategies we might employ. You might want to refer back again at Chapter 5 which looked at not only the behaviour management approaches that can be employed when teaching physical education, but also other health and safety considerations we need to take into account when planning lessons.

Having started to focus on our organisation, we now need to think about how we will present our lesson and what teaching approaches we intend to use. If you refer back to Chapter 3 you will remember that different teaching approaches allow us to develop skills across domains of learning. If we utilise the teaching styles of Mosston and Ashworth (1994) we can start to ask similar questions to those we have thought about previously in this chapter.

 Task 8.3

Look at the learning objectives for our lesson.

- To be able to send and receive the ball over different distances showing accuracy
- To develop the ability to play small-sided games
- To be able to review your own performance and identify ways of improving

  1 What teaching approaches do you feel are most appropriate for these activities (remember you can use different approaches for different activities)?
  2 Where possible, share these ideas with a partner. What are the similarities and differences?

The learning objectives require us to provide pupils with the opportunity to practise a specific skill – sending and receiving the ball. This suggests that we are looking at using a reproductive style, most probably the practice style, although we could consider the reciprocal style particularly as we are looking at accuracy and direction in our learning objectives as well. There is also a need to include an opportunity for evaluation and feedback.

Having chosen our teaching approaches we can start to think more about the actual content: what we are going to be doing in each part of the lesson.

We introduced the concept of starter activities earlier in this chapter. Such activities should provide a link for pupils between what they learnt in their previous lesson and what they are going to work on during the current lesson. They engage pupils from the start of the lesson and should allow pupils to gain an understanding of the learning objectives for the lesson. For example, in physical education we might engage them in a warm-up activity, but in doing so ask them to think about specific skills that they have learnt.

Having started the lesson with some form of starter activity we now need to have a smooth transition into our next activity. We need to be clear how the starter activity relates to the main body of the lesson. We also need to consider how activities should be differentiated to support the whole class (Chapter 4 and the companion website provide further details on these). As we move through the lesson we need to consider opportunities for assessment.

'Assessment covers all those activities which are undertaken by teachers and others to measure the effectiveness of teaching and learning' (Haydn, 2005: 301). Such a definition provides us with the three key points of assessment: that it is an active process, that it is undertaken by a range of individuals, and that there must be clear criteria on which judgements or observations are made. When choosing to assess, we need to be clear about its purpose. For example, are we using assessment to inform us or our pupils (formative assessment), which would require us to engage in assessment throughout the lesson; or to summarise the learning that has taken place (summative assessment), which suggests that the assessment takes place at the end of a learning process?

Three main types of assessment are commonly associated with education: norm referenced, criterion referenced and ipsative. When using norm referencing we are looking at comparing our pupils against each other. An example in physical education may be when we are engaging them in some form of timed event, where we identify the fastest and consequently the slowest pupil. While such a process allows us to rank pupils, the associated impact can be detrimental to the development of pupils' self-esteem (see Chapter 2).

A more appropriate approach may be that of criterion-referenced assessment. Here assessment is based upon achievement against specific criteria. If we think about our current lesson, we are looking at pupils being able to perform specific skills and therefore we need to provide them with the criteria (learning or teaching points) to be able to perform the skill. These then become our criteria for assessment.

A further type of assessment that we may wish to use is ipsative assessment. This is sometimes referred to as value-added assessment. Here the focus is on the individual (pupil) assessing their own progress against themselves. In such a way they are able to identify what they were able to do at, for example, the start of the lesson, and then at the end of the lesson to gauge the progress they have made. Such an approach reflects recent governmental policy around the process of assessment for learning which encourages pupils to gain an understanding of what they have already learnt, what they need to do next and how they might achieve this.

In our planning we need to be considering how and when we can build in opportunities for pupils to assess themselves or each other, asking ourselves how we as teachers will engage in assessment. At the end of the lesson we need to consider how we provide pupils with opportunities to reflect upon their learning.

Earlier in the chapter we identified that at the start of the lesson you would have provided an overview of the learning objectives. At the end of the lesson you need to provide pupils with an opportunity to identify their level of success against these criteria as well as think about what they would need to do to improve further.

 Task 8.4

1 Spend some time thinking and researching the different methods of assessment that can be employed within the primary classroom.
2 Identify those with which you are familiar and consider how you may use such approaches within your physical education lessons.

How will you know you are achieving your aims?

Having planned and implemented your lesson you now need to reflect upon the extent to which you achieved your aims. Some of this reflection will take place during the lesson itself as you modify your lesson to reflect pupils' progress (do not think that you have to stick to every detail of your lesson plan – if something is going really well or particularly badly, work around it).

Amos and Postlethwaite argue that reflection is important as it allows the individual to:

> practise a way of thinking about teaching which will enable them to keep their knowledge updated by reference to changing circumstances, and to changing awareness of the formal theories and research as that develops. (1996: 14)

Schon (1983) identifies two types of reflection:

- reflection in action, which occurs while you are doing the activity (during the lesson)
- reflection of action, which occurs once something has been done (at the end of the lesson).

So what do we reflect on? Ideally we want to reflect upon the learning objectives. To what extent did pupils achieve the learning objectives? What were the strengths and weaknesses of the lesson, in other words what went well and what do I need to improve next time? Avoid the temptation to always focus on the negative. Bailey (2006) suggests the focus should be around the content, organisation and presentation of the lesson. You should use the results of your evaluation to identify where you are going next. This is the time to either plan the next lesson or at least jot down a few ideas to use as a basis. By doing this you are already thinking about the next lesson in the scheme and can either plan it straight away or at least make some notes to come back to later.

As well as evaluating your own teaching, during your initial teacher education programme you will also be evaluated against your teaching standards. Thus when planning your lesson, you also need to consider how you will demonstrate attainment against your specific standard. Professionally you should therefore keep abreast of any changes to the standards so that you clearly understand what you are expected to have achieved against each standard.

 Task 8.5

1 During your initial teacher education programme you will engage in a range of evaluation situations. During one placement try and have your lesson videoed (you will need to check with your school if this is possible as it has potential issues associated with safeguarding pupils). Having completed an initial evaluation of your lesson, watch the video of your lesson and complete a second evaluation based on what you have observed.

   a What differences have you noted?
   b How will your teaching change as a result of this?

2 Try and observe other staff (this could be a fellow student) with whom you work and with their permission complete an evaluation of their lesson.

   a What do you notice about the way they deliver their sessions?
   b What can you take away from your observations?

 Chapter summary

The aim of this chapter has been to develop your knowledge and understanding of the planning process in physical education. While much of what you have read will support your existing knowledge of the planning process you may wish to reflect upon the following review questions.

1 What key factors do you need to consider when planning a physical education lesson?
2 What constitutes an effective lesson?
3 How will you include assessment within your lesson planning?
4 Why, how and when should you evaluate your lesson?

Further reading

Cockburn, A.D. and Handscomb, G. (eds) (2006) *Teaching children 3 to 11*, 2nd edn. London: Paul Chapman Publishing.

The text provides guidance and support for those engaging in training and development associated with the primary phase of education. As well as looking at aspects of teaching and learning, it also focuses on developing reflective practice.

Metzler, M.W. (2005) *Instructional models for physical education*, 2nd edn. Arizona: Holcomb Hathaway Inc.

Pickup, I., Price, L., Shaughnessy, J., Spence, J. and Trace, M. (2008). *Learning to teach primary PE*. Exeter: Learning Matters.

This compact text provides further support for the planning of physical education learning experiences, as well as exploring the content of physical education in primary schools.

CHAPTER 9

PROMOTING PHYSICAL EDUCATION ACROSS THE CURRICULUM

Chapter aims

- To develop a greater understanding of how physical education can be used to enhance learning across the curriculum
- To develop an understanding of cross-curricular themes evident within the school environment
- To provide a range of practical activities designed to support cross-subject and cross-curricular learning

Previous chapters have looked at the role of physical education in developing pupils' competences across a range of physical activities. However, in defining physical education in Chapter 1, we acknowledged that physical education was more than just being physically active. Chapter 2 looked at the processes associated with learning and how physical education may contribute to an individual's development across the different learning domains. The purpose of this chapter is to draw on these two chapters further to acknowledge the breadth of learning opportunities physical education has the potential to offer for the development and application of knowledge, skills and understanding across curriculum subjects, and of key themes or skills evident in curriculum design.

From its inception the National Curriculum has encouraged the development of learning across the curriculum, including the promotion of: pupils' spiritual, moral, social and cultural development; citizenship; key communication, numeracy and ICT skills; working with others; improving one's own learning and problem-solving; and thinking skills. Recent changes have focused upon the cross-curricular aspect of provision of general teaching requirements such as inclusion (see Chapter 4), the use of ICT, the use of language, health and safety aspects (see Chapter 5) and the promotion of spiritual, moral, social and cultural aspects. By completing Task 9.1, you can begin to think about these in more depth.

 Task 9.1

1 Using your teaching placements or current teaching timetable as a point of reference, identify subjects where physical education might be able to make a contribution.
2 For each subject try to identify examples of activities that could be undertaken in physical education which would allow pupils to consolidate and apply existing knowledge. You may wish to think about creating a portfolio in which to store these.
3 Share these with a colleague.

Physical education and the core curriculum subjects

If you have completed Task 9.1, you will have already started to think about curriculum subjects that can be integrated with physical education. For example, if we look at science, one activity that you might have considered looking at is the heart and the impact of exercise on the heart (we will look at this activity in much more depth later in the chapter). For mathematics you could consider activities such as data collection through athletic events, or the use of measuring skills. For English or literacy-based activities we can identify activities such as writing, for example writing a match report. These are just a few examples of how curriculum requirements within physical education can be used to support other aspects of the curriculum. Task 9.2 provides you with an opportunity to look at this in much more depth.

Task 9.2

1 Using the current programmes of study for Foundation Stage, Key Stage 1 and Key Stage 2 (those of you who are working with different curricula should access you own guidance materials) identify any examples of core curriculum content that could be taught in that subject and in physical education.
2 Compile a table demonstrating where similarities occur.
3 Think about how you might integrate these into your current teaching.

By completing Task 9.2, you should have identified a number of examples where curriculum content is taught through physical education and at least one other subject area. For example, knowledge and understanding associated with healthy and active lifestyles can be taught in physical education and science. However, we will start by looking at the example of the heart and the impact of exercise on it which we mentioned earlier in this chapter.

Physical education and science

During early stages of development pupils should be encouraged to develop their knowledge and understanding of health and growth. As part of this they need to know that exercise is necessary to maintain a healthy lifestyle. If we reflect on how physical education can be used to develop pupils' knowledge and understanding of fitness and health we can clearly identify an opportunity for integration within the curriculum. However, we need to be clear about how this would look in practice.

When we get pupils to warm up we can encourage them to think about what is happening to their body as their level of activity increases. The key issue is for pupils to understand that there will be changes to their body, but that this is normal. As they move, they can be encouraged to think about what is happening to their:

- heart – it starts to beat faster; 'I feel a thumping in my chest'
- breathing – 'I breathe more'
- muscles – 'I get tired'
- colour – 'I go red'
- temperature – 'I get hotter'.

They can be asked to share their ideas with each other, thereby encouraging the development of communication skills (again we will look at this in more detail as we move through the chapter). This is only one example; further practical activities can be found throughout the chapter as well as on the companion website.

General aspects of health and well-being that pupils are encouraged to learn include:

- that to stay healthy we need an adequate and varied diet
- how to present information about diet and health
- that we need exercise to stay healthy and maintain our muscles
- that when we exercise, our muscles work harder
- how to measure pulse rate and relate it to heart beat
- how to identify factors which could affect pulse rate and make predictions about changes
- that when humans exercise, muscles move parts of the skeleton and this activity requires an increased blood supply, so the heart beat increases and the pulse rate is faster. (QCDA, 2010b)

Within a physical education context we can start to look at muscles and different exercises that can be used to stretch and strengthen them (see the companion website for a range of examples). Pupils can be encouraged to start to use appropriate terminology for the main muscle groups as they warm up (this again links to the development of literacy and language skills which we will look at in more detail later in the chapter). As they warm up we can also get them to think about muscles and bones and their roles in supporting the body. In looking at developing their understanding of pulse and heartbeat, they can be set short challenges that require them to record their pulse after different activities, for example jogging on the spot for a set period, completing a specified distance, or completing a series of specific skills such as step-ups. Later in the chapter we will explore how such activities can also be used to support knowledge development across the use of ICT as well as knowledge and understanding of the use and interpretation of data.

? Task 9.3

1 Identify a set of key scientific terms that you wish pupils to learn and use during your lessons. For each one produce some form of resource that will allow pupils to develop an understanding of:

a the term itself (a definition)
b some form of practical application of the term (for example a picture)

c examples of when the term might be used (a model of the word within a sentence).

2 Plan an opportunity within your own teaching when you can use these resources and evaluate their success. Where necessary modify these resources for future use. These resources can then be added to your portfolio.

Physical education and mathematics (numeracy)

If we now look at how physical education can be used to promote knowledge and understanding of mathematical principles, again clear parallels can be drawn. During the early stages of their development pupils are expected to develop knowledge, skills and understanding of the use and application of number, as well as shapes, spaces and measurements. If we focus initially on the use and application of number, we can look at aspects such as counting. Warm-up activities can be used to engage pupils in counting, for example a number is called out and pupils form a group of that number to get into the appropriate group size. Simple activities such as counting the number of throws they complete in a set time or identifying when they have completed a set number can also be encouraged. Further activities can be set up so that they have to solve a problem at the end, for example pupils complete a simple orienteering course and at each control have to solve a simple mathematical problem (see the companion website support material for Chapter 7). A further application of number in physical education is data collection and pupils can be encouraged to collect data regarding an activity, for example their times for running or their pulse after different activities. They can then use this data to produce graphs and charts allowing them to share their ideas with others. We will look at this in more depth in the section on developing ICT skills.

Looking at the knowledge, skills and understanding associated with shape, space and measures, pupils can be engaged in using equipment to measure the distance they have jumped, or the time it took them to complete a set distance. Again this data can be used to develop numeracy skills. As with physical education and science, key terminology can be used to support learning, and again you might find it beneficial to produce a resource which focuses on the use of key mathematical terms. Through gymnastic and dance activities, pupils can be encouraged to explore aspects of movement, including direction of travel, and different types of movement such as rotation. They can explore the different shapes they might make with their bodies when performing gymnastic movements (you may wish to refer back to Chapter 6 for further examples) and can also be encouraged to think about the different shapes they make on the floor during their routines.

Task 9.4

1 Look at the examples introduced of developing mathematical principles and physical education. Identify a range of activities that you could integrate into your physical education lessons that would allow pupils to develop their knowledge, skills and understanding of numbers and shape, space and measure.
2 When you plan your next week of lessons, identify specifically how physical education lessons will build on the knowledge, skills and understanding developed in mathematics/numeracy lessons.
3 Share these ideas with colleagues and integrate them into your portfolio as appropriate.

Physical education and English (literacy and communication skills)

During early childhood the development of skills associated with speaking, listening, group work, drama and the use of language are encouraged. Applying this to the requirements of physical education we can see that the subject allows pupils to develop communicative skills through speaking, particularly if they are reflecting on the activity they have just completed, and the associated need to listen to feedback and the opinions of others.

Drama activities can be encouraged through dance and gymnastic activities whereby pupils may be encouraged to tell a story through the sequences they perform. Storyboards can be used to allow pupils to organise their thoughts and produce a focused sequence. They can then be used as a prompt to support their explanation of the sequence, as well as a basis for feedback from other pupils. Again the use of appropriate language is to be encouraged in the way pupils describe things as well as how they give feedback.

In combining writing with physical education, pupils can use physical activities as content for stories or reports. Linking back to the Sport Education teaching approach discussed in Chapter 3, pupils can be encouraged to write match reports, write up their coaching sessions or even review their own performance. In this way, pupils are being encouraged to use contextualised data that potentially has a higher personal value to them.

Physical education and other curriculum subjects

So far we have focused on what are commonly referred to as the core subjects within the National Curriculum and identified a range of activities that can be integrated into planning to develop skills linking physical education to other curriculum areas. The next section looks at how we can use physical education as a vehicle to deliver or enhance other aspects of curriculum subject areas using specific examples from geography and music.

Physical education and geography

While the teaching of OAA is not statutory within curriculum documentation, opportunities for the development of children's geographical skills are evident, such as route planning and map-making. This can be achieved in a practical manner by pupils drawing simple maps of the gym and then designing a simple orienteering course. As pupils progress, simple problem-solving activities can be introduced which encourage the development of more complex skills associated with the use of maps and decision-making skills (a range of examples can be found in the companion website material for Chapter 7).

Physical education and music

During the early stages of development pupils are expected to be taught to 'explore and express their ideas and feelings using movement, dance and expressive and musical language' and in doing so should be able to 'make improvements to their own work' (QCA, 1999a: 16). Chapter 7 looked at the development of concepts, skills and processes and the teaching of dance-based activities and these can be used as a conduit for the development of such music and dance-related skills. For example, pupils might be given a theme or story and use dance movements to tell their tale. They might be given simple rhythms to move to, or different styles of music which require them to express their interpretations of that music.

It is clear that synergies exist across curriculum subjects and by demonstrating the interrelated nature of aspects of what they are taught children can see how their knowledge can be transferred across different contexts. This increases the potential for the rehearsal and application of their skills which can deepen their overall learning experiences.

Physical education and other aspects of primary education

The first part of this chapter has focused on developing your knowledge and understanding of how physical education can be used to deliver aspects of other curriculum areas. What we have not yet focused upon are those skills associated with personal, social and health education. These will be looked at in more detail as we move through the next section of this chapter.

If we think back to Chapter 1, which looked at defining education and physical education, and Chapter 3, which looked at learning and the domains of learning, we identified that education is more than just focusing on the development of subject knowledge. We will now start to focus on some important aspects of primary education aside from subject-specific teaching. These include the inclusion of all learners (see Chapter 4), the use of ICT, language usage (while we have covered aspects of this earlier in the chapter with respect to primary English, we will explore this in further detail within this section), aspects of health and safety (see Chapter 5), and pupils' moral and spiritual development which can include learning and thinking skills, personal and emotional skills and social skills.

ICT capability

Within this curriculum area, the focus is placed on pupils' ability to develop their existing knowledge of ICT and apply it to different contexts, acknowledging as they do the impact this may have. Specific skills pupils are expected to develop include the following:

- The ability to search for and select relevant information – in a physical education context, pupils can be encouraged to find information relating to the performance of a specific skill, activity or sporting event (World Cup, Olympic Games). This could then be used to support an individual or class project.
- The ability to create, manipulate and process information – this second point emphasises data generation and information processing. The focus here should be on the collection of individual data rather than group data which, if not handled sensitively, may raise potential issues around comparisons between pupils. If we think back to earlier in the chapter when we looked at the integration of science with physical education via a focus on healthy living, we considered collecting information regarding changes in pulse rate from different types of activities. By requiring pupils to record such data, they can start to analyse their own information to make predictions as well as use the data to form graphical representations of changes that may have occurred. Similar data can be collected through athletic activities, and in this way pupils are not only developing ICT skills but also working to develop skills associated with mathematics.

- The ability to review their own work and offer suggests as to how improvements can be made – the emphasis is on the use of feedback to make improvements. In general, feedback within a physical education context has a tendency to be generated from the information given by others, for example on pupils' ability to perform a specific skill the quality of a piece of work. Advances in technology, however, now provide opportunities for individuals to generate their own feedback. Many schools now have handheld video cameras which allow immediate playback. In physical education these can be used in activities such as gymnastics and athletics to video individual performance. The performance can then be reviewed by the performer, allowing them to analyse their own performance against specific criteria (for example teaching points) and suggest ways in which performance can be improved. As with any use of capture data, for example photographs and video, consideration needs to be given to how the data is then stored or destroyed (again you will need to make reference to any safeguarding pupils policy).

 Task 9.5

1 Spend some time collating the information provided on developing ICT capability in physical education.
2 Identify a range of activities you intend to integrate into your own teaching.
3 When possible deliver these ideas and evaluate their effectiveness.
4 Identify any changes you might make subsequent to your initial delivery, and add your completed examples to your portfolio.

Learning and thinking skills

Learning and thinking skills place an emphasis on pupils developing their ability to learn (you may wish to reread Chapter 2 to refresh your memory) and to think creatively. They are also concerned with generating ideas and problem solving. This area can be divided into the following categories.

Investigating

Developing pupils' investigative skills can start with basic problem-solving activities. Chapter 6 looked at the development of fundamental motor skills including encouraging pupils to explore different ways of performing skills, for example getting them to think about what different body parts might do to contribute to the performance of the skills. This can also contribute to developing their understanding of the impact of exercise on their bodies. Chapter 7 looked at concepts associated with the development of strategic and tactical awareness. A vital part of this process is encouraging pupils to investigate a range of methods before deciding upon a preferred approach.

Creativity and development

In fostering creativity, we are encouraging pupils to look at different ways to use the skills they have across different contexts. Using gymnastic activities as an example, we can consider using warm-up exercises to encourage pupils to think about different body parts they might use to move in different ways or different types of balancing they might perform. They can then be encouraged to choose some of these to integrate into longer gymnastic sequences.

Communication

We looked in detail at the development of communication skills when we explored integrating English and literacy with physical education earlier in this chapter. When exploring communication in physical education we need to consider how children deliver feedback to each other and the impact this feedback may have, as well as the visual, written and verbal ways in which they communicate. We will look at this in more depth in the section on the development of personal, emotional and social skills.

Evaluation

Encouraging pupils to develop evaluative skills can be done by integrating a range of approaches. It is important that pupils have a clear understanding of what they are evaluating and against what criteria; consequently we need to consider in some depth how we introduce and support skill development in this area. For example, we need to provide clear criteria against which pupils will evaluate performance. This could be in the use of specific resources cards generated through the use of reciprocal teaching approaches. We also need to get pupils to consider how they use the information they generate as a result of evaluation. Consideration therefore may need to be given to encouraging pupils to set specific goals. Figure 9.1 provides an example of how this might be achieved.

A similar checklist can be generated for all skills allowing pupils to manage their own learning and we look at this in more depth below. This technique allows pupils to review the progress they are making, encouraging them to set specific goals. In many ways this mirrors approaches they might have experienced in curriculum areas such as English and mathematics where they are encouraged to log their own progress.

Personal and emotional skills

It is important to encourage children to take an increasing level of responsibility for their own learning. In doing so they can develop confidence and

Skill: Throw
Key points
What I did well (what went well – WWW)
What I need to do better (even better if – EBI)
What I need to do next
What improvements I made

Figure 9.1 Skill evaluation proforma

resilience. In many ways the skills they are developing within this area mirror many of those we have already explored and specifically relate to aspects of learning evident within the affective domain (see Chapter 2). In terms of specific skills pupils are encouraged to identify their strengths, manage their feelings, take part in reflection, goal setting and independent working, and develop control over their own physical skills and movements (QCDA, 2010a).

Identifying strengths

Some of the practical examples of activities discussed earlier in this chapter can be used to allow pupils to identify their own strengths. If we refer back to Figure 9.1 we can clearly see that the aim of the proforma is to provide pupils with the opportunity to evaluate their performance allowing them to identify not only their strengths, but also areas requiring further development as well as activities that would allow them to make improvements (goal setting).

Developing and managing feelings

As we have previously identified, the visual nature of physical education means that it has the capacity to impact on the social development of individuals as they make comparisons between themselves and others. The complexity of the skills that pupils are expected to develop can cause frustration, in particular if they are struggling to complete the activity or not making as much progress as their peers.

 Task 9.6

1 Identify a recent time when you have become frustrated with yourself.
2 What was your reaction to this frustration?
3 What were the consequences of your reaction?
4 If the situation was repeated would you react differently?

As Task 9.6 demonstrates, at times we all become frustrated and will react to situations in different ways. This may be a result of prior experience, so our reaction is based on a previous outcome, or it may be a result of how we were feeling at the time; if it had happened at another time our reaction could have been different. Despite being adults, there will be times when childlike instincts surface; as such we need to appreciate that pupils in the early stages of development may not have the level of maturity necessary to make correct judgments about their own reactions. Consideration therefore needs to be given to the emotional support structures that can be integrated into lessons. For example, if a pupil is becoming frustrated at not being able to perform a specific skill, there may be a way in which the activity can be modified to allow them to experience success. This could include a change in equipment or a change in the task being completed. It is important to create a learning environment in which pupils feel confident enough to seek help and support. Conversely pupils may become frustrated with each other because they are not all working at the same level and as a result start to blame each other for poor performances. Sadly on too many occasions we see frustrations being played out on the sports field and then replicated in the school playground!

In completing Task 9.6, you would have identified some reaction mechanisms that occur when you vent your own frustrations. As we as adults have a level of maturity not evident in pupils we need to provide children with opportunities to develop their own understanding of reactions and the consequences of their actions and to develop an ability to manage their own behaviour. Chapter 4 looked at engaging with inclusion in physical education teaching. Some schools work closely with pupils to identify exit strategies from situations, for example pupils are able to identify when they are becoming frustrated and then remove themselves from the situation until they have calmed down. You should consult the school's policy regarding such practice. It is important that within any school the approach is applied consistently. You might wish to revisit Chapters 2, 4 and 5 where behaviour management strategies are covered in more detail.

Developing reflection

Throughout this book we have made reference to the provision of and processes associated with developing pupils' ability to reflect upon their own and others, performances. A key part of this is children's ability to evaluate their own performance and use such evaluations to inform subsequent performance. Earlier in this chapter we identified how reflection can be supported by the use ICT. Pupils may also engage in individual action planning, for example identifying what they need to do to improve and how this might be achieved. The process of reflection can also be used to support pupils identified as gifted and talented (see Chapter 4) and thereby allow for accelerated learning opportunities to be integrated into lesson planning (see Chapter 8). It is important that pupils are clear about the criteria on which they are basing any assessment, and feed back using appropriate terminology.

 Task 9.7

1   Review your physical education lesson plans for the last term.
2   Identify within them when opportunities arose that required pupils to reflect upon their own performance.
3   Identify a list of potential activities that can now be integrated into your planning to engage pupils in regular review opportunities.

Goal setting

In setting goals, we are encouraging pupils to develop more responsibility for their own learning. The proforma in Figure 9.1 requires pupils to identify activities that they need to undertake to make further progress. We need to consider the timescale of goals, for example at the start of a lesson pupils may be encouraged to identify what it is they want to achieve by the end of the lesson or even during an activity. Taking a practical example from athletics: in developing pupils' ability to run at speed, pupils can be encouraged to identify a target distance they think they could achieve in a specified period of time. For example, they could place a cone at the distance they think they will reach in five seconds. They can then be timed by a partner to test whether they can achieve the predicted distance.

Another form of goal setting is based around levels of attainment. This engages pupils in developing an understanding of the level at which they are currently working, and from here identifying what they would need to achieve to move up to the next level and how this might be achieved.

Social skills

Developing social skills places an emphasis on how individuals work together and again physical education offers a range of opportunities for this to occur. Much of the practical work associated with the subject requires pupils to work collaboratively towards an end goal. In many of the activities undertaken, success is a reflection of the team work in which the individuals engage. Individual skills that contribute to this development include being able to listen and respond appropriately, adapt behaviour for different situations, work collaboratively towards common goals, take turns, share, negotiate, and give constructive support and feedback.

Listening and responding
Listening and responding are directly linked with literacy skills and focus on how pupils communicate with each other as well as with you the teacher. In physical education there is a range of opportunities across different contexts for pupils to engage in activities that cultivate these skills. In all lessons pupils will be expected to listen to instructions. These could be delivered by the class teacher or, dependent upon the teaching approaches being adopted, by the pupils themselves. Pupils should therefore spend time learning how to listen. For many they will hear the instruction being given, but being able to make sense of such instructions may be more problematic. No doubt we can all recall instances when we have given instructions and thought that all the pupils understood what they had been asked to do, only to realise as they move off to do the activity that actually they did not understand at all! While we can put this down to experience, we need to realise that at times we may need to engage some form of checking mechanism, for example 'Does everyone understand?' 'Has anyone got any questions?' 'Can you repeat back to me the instructions that I've just given you?' If you think back to Chapter 4 and the use of questioning, you can see that in developing pupils' ability to listen, we will also need to reflect on our own ability to question.

Listening to instructions is just one part of a wide range of listening opportunities in physical education as pupils will need to listen to a range of individuals including their peers. We have talked a lot about the use of feedback and how pupils use the feedback they receive to improve their own performance.

Pupils need to be aware not only of how they give feedback, but also of how they interpret the feedback they are being given. It is therefore important to get pupils to draw out the key points from the information they are being given. If we refer to Figure 9.1 we can see that it provides an opportunity for pupils to note key points, again developing their ability to listen and draw out key points.

Pupils might also undertake leadership roles which require them to listen to a range of ideas offered by their peers before deciding upon a strategy. In this scenario not only are they developing listening skills, but they also have to think about how they respond to such ideas.

In the context of physical education the development of pupils' ability to respond will be determined by how they interpret instructions, for example in OAA they might be given a series of simple instructions and equipment and then have to develop a strategy for completing the task (see Chapter 7 for an overview of delivering OAA in physical education). However, they will also need to develop the ability to respond to different ideas from different people, particularly if they are presented with a leadership role. In trying to develop one specific skill, advances in others may also occur. For example, in attempting to develop pupils' listening and responding skills, we are likely to also be working on their learning and thinking skills as well as their personal and emotional skills.

Adapting behaviour and working collaboratively

As part of developing social skills pupils need to develop an understanding of how their behaviour may impact on others as well as ability to take increasing responsibility for their own actions. Putting this into a physical education context we can start to think about the different roles pupils may undertake and how this may impact on the behaviour they exhibit. A good example of this is to consider the Sport Education model that was introduced in Chapter 3.

The focus of learning in the Sport Education model is on the use of a productive pedagogical approach which engages pupils in a range of roles and responsibilities, for example team captain, coach, referee. At the heart of this approach (see Metzler, 2005) lies the development not only of physical skills relating to physical education, but also of the affective domain of learning, including pupils' abilities to undertake a range of sport-related roles and to work collaboratively within these roles. In this context pupils will start to exhibit behaviours relevant to the different roles they adopt. For example, you may expect a pupil who is taking on a leadership role to exhibit different behaviours from those who are taking on a more participatory role. If you want to see this in context, at the next training day you attend watch how different people with different levels of responsibility behave.

In the section on developing ICT capability we gave examples of how we could analyse performance in a range of activities. This can also be applied to analysing behaviour, for example pupils could be encouraged to be videoed working with others to identify their strengths and weaknesses. In doing so they could begin to understand how their behaviour impacts upon others and this process could be used to suggest improvements that could be made. This is particularly important if pupils are undertaking some form of leadership role and working with young pupils, for example as playground supervisors.

In providing learning opportunities for pupils to work together collaboratively consideration needs to be given to the appropriateness of the activities as well as the state of readiness to learn. Activities should be developed progressively, allowing pupils to take increasing responsibility for the outcomes. You may wish at this point to refresh your understanding of the theories and processes of learning in Chapter 2, as well as the approaches to the teaching of physical education in Chapter 3.

This chapter has focused on some of the more generic educational skills covered in the wider curriculum and how physical education can be used to develop cross-curricular learning. It is clear that different types of skills are connected and development in one area will lead to development in another, for example evaluative skills (which include evaluation and reflection) can be developed through literacy, numeracy, ICT capability, learning and thinking skills, and personal and social skills. You should now attempt Task 9.8 to further embed your knowledge.

 Task 9.8

Using all that you have read in this chapter, identify a range of activities that could be integrated into your physical education teaching to provide pupils with the opportunity to develop skills across the curriculum.

 Chapter summary

This chapter has investigated a range of activities that can be used to promote physical education across other curriculum subject areas. It is clear that common knowledge, skills and understanding exist between subjects and that if we are to engage pupils and enhance their learning experiences, we should be exploring ways of providing opportunities for them to apply their skills across different contexts. To review your learning you should complete the review questions below.

1 What is your personal rationale for promoting physical education across the curriculum?
2 What would you identify as the key skills pupils should be required to develop across all curriculum subjects?
3 What changes are you going to make to your own teaching to integrate a higher level of cross-curricular and cross-subject teaching?

Further reading

Barnes, J. (2011) *Cross-curricular learning 3–14*, (2nd edn). London: Sage.
This textbook provides an overview of a range of strategies that can be applied when looking to promote cross-curricular links.

Lawrence, J. (2004) 'Key skills: developing transferable skills across the curriculum', in S. Capel, R. Heilbronn, M. Leask and T. Turner (eds), *Starting to Teach in the Secondary School*. Abingdon: RoutledgeFalmer. pp. 49–60.
This chapter focuses on how key skills can be developed across the curriculum. Case studies provide the opportunity for you to reflect upon your own practice.

CHAPTER 10

PHYSICAL EDUCATION AND THE WIDER COMMUNITY

Chapter aims

- To review how physical education in primary schools can be supported by the wider community
- To identify potential external providers and how they can contribute to physical education within the primary school

Physical education has always been supported by the wider community. All primary schools will have associated secondary schools where pupils transfer at the end of their primary education. Local authorities provide facilities to support physical activity, for example local sports centres. Some organisations have sports development officers. These might be employed by the local education authorities or an equivalent organisation and may be linked to specific governing bodies. You are also likely to find that local clubs and organisations offer links into junior provision within their own structures.

With the advent of extended schools and other policy changes, there has been an increase in the number and range of external providers of physical education. It is therefore important to look at how physical education contributes to the wider community as well as identifying parameters for engaging with external providers. Completing Task 10.1 should allow you to start thinking about the opportunities that exist within your community.

 Task 10.1

1 Produce an audit of the local sports clubs and facilities located close to your school.
2 For each one, identify a key point of contact and the opportunities they can provide.
3 Produce a display for pupils outlining the opportunities that exist within their locality for participating in sport and physical activity outside of the school curriculum.

Completing Task 10.1 should help you to identify the wealth of opportunities that lie outside of the school classroom for pupils to participate in. Most sports clubs and associations will have teams and activities appropriate for primary school children and many will be keen to engage with schools to promote themselves and provide opportunities for your pupils. If you are fortunate enough to live in a city with professional sports clubs then it is likely that they will have dedicated employees with specified roles focusing on engagement with schools and the provision of training opportunities. Your local authority may have a designated sports development team, with a remit to organise sports tournaments for pupils. Additionally, you may be linked to a school sports college where opportunities for inter-school competitions exist.

The range of opportunities available can be very broad, and deciding on who and what to be involved with can become problematic. Chapter 11 looks at the role of the subject leader in identifying and working with external organisations. It is important that engagement with external organisations offers an extension to the opportunities provided within the curriculum and does not become a substitute.

We will now look in a little more detail at the range of opportunities you might engage in, focusing on working with your secondary school, using your local facilities and working with external providers.

Working with your secondary school

Chapter 1 looked at some of the recent initiatives implemented in schools. One example was the establishment of the School Sports programmes. One important aspect of this initiative is the establishment of closer physical education links between primary and secondary schools through the work of a school sports co-ordinator, usually employed by the secondary school, and primary link tutors based within the primary school. This has given rise to increased interaction between schools and the opportunity for pupils in primary schools to experience some teaching from secondary-trained staff and to access secondary school facilities and equipment.

However, the development of close links between primary and secondary schools is also important to facilitate the transition across phases of education which occurs when pupils leave the primary phase of education at the age of eleven. Research (Capel et al., 2003; Capel et al., 2004; Capel et al., 2007) identifies that the transition from primary to secondary school can be problematic for some pupils. Changes in approaches to teaching, characterised by a move from pupil-centred teaching in primary schools to a more subject-focused approach in secondary schools, as well as structural and organisational changes such as the change from staying in the same class for most subjects to moving classes for each subject, can impact on a child's attainment, motivation and self-esteem.

Within physical education the transition to secondary education can lead to a decline in levels of attainment, characterised by a tendency of staff to adopt a 'fresh start approach' (Lawrence, 2006). This occurs when staff choose to ignore the prior learning of pupils as they lack confidence in what has taken place in the primary school, for example they may choose to re-teach the fundamental movement skills at the start of pupils' secondary education. Developing closer links with secondary schools through regular meetings and sharing curriculum content, planning and teaching opportunities will foster a greater level of understanding of pupils' prior learning and promote continuity and progression in learning across age phases.

Within your school, there will be a designated staff member with responsibility for liaising with secondary schools, and it will be beneficial for you to spend some time discussing the transfer arrangements and links that exist between you and secondary schools. This is outlined in Task 10.2.

 Task 10.2

Working with you school transfer co-ordinator discuss the following.

1 What links currently exist between your primary and secondary school in relation to physical education?
2 Is there any shared practice in respect of the planning and teaching of physical education?
3 Is any information shared between your primary and secondary school in relation to attainment and curriculum content in physical education?
4 What improvements (if any) could be made to the links that exist?

Working with local facilities

Many primary schools are limited in the range of facilities available for delivering high quality physical education and school sport. For example, few schools still have a swimming pool and those that do tend to have an outdoor facility that will not be available throughout the whole school year. As you know from Chapter 7, swimming is an integral aspect of the physical education curriculum and it is highly likely that you will need to attend a local pool as part of your teaching. Health and safety aspects related to aquatic activities will need to be considered (see Chapter 5) and it is also likely that you will need to use specialist staff to support you in delivering these sessions (we look at the use of external providers later in this chapter).

However, we should not restrict ourselves to using leisure facilities for only aquatic-based activities. It may be that you can access a sports hall either at a leisure centre or at your local secondary school. In doing so you can start to increase the range of activities pupils experience. Using facilities at a secondary school to which pupils from your primary school transfer provides further opportunities for developing links and as a result offers pupils the chance to familiarise themselves with these surroundings lessening the impact of when they transfer out of primary education.

In Chapter 7 we explored aspects of OAA. Local playing fields provide extended opportunities for engagement in orienteering-based activities and increased space for games or athletic activities. When using such spaces you will need to take into account that the general public might also access the provision at the same time. You will therefore need to consider the safeguarding of pupils as well as health and safety issues associated with using communal environments.

Working with external providers

You may also consider working with local external providers to enhance educational provision. Such providers might include local sports clubs and their coaches, local initial teacher educators or external physical education providers. It is important to ensure that this collaboration enhances pupils' experiences. Chapter 1 looked at the role and values of physical education and identified what underpins high quality physical education and school sport, as well as exploring the difference between sport and physical education. Regardless of our position within a school we have a responsibility for the quality of provision. Recent changes in educational policy concerning protected preparation time and the development of school sports colleges has given rise to an increased range of external providers going into schools and in some cases delivering physical education lessons. It is essential that any individual delivering the curriculum is competent and confident in curriculum planning, assessment and evaluation processes. In essence they must have a clear understanding of the curriculum in its entirety.

Overall responsibility for the delivery of the curriculum lies with the school and subject leader and therefore both have a responsibility to quality assure provision. Organisations such as the Association for Physical Education (AfPE) have worked hard to establish kitemarks which identify those providers who have achieved a recognised level of quality. Guidance is available from local authorities as well as publications Whitlam and Beaumont (2008) identify four key areas for consideration when engaging with anyone in delivering physical education:

1   quality of relationships
2   knowledge of pupils and their development
3   management of learning
4   knowledge of the activities being undertaken.

 Task 10.3

1   Identify any external individuals (including support staff) who have supported or might support you in the delivery of physical education lessons.
2   What information do you think your school should have regarding their suitability to deliver the activity?
3   How would you go about accessing such information?

Safeguarding pupils

When using external organisations and facilities the safeguarding of pupils is a priority. As with any staff member, appropriate checks need to be conducted on any individual who may come into contact with pupils. Accordingly any external individual should be checked in line with school and governmental policy. Checks need to be undertaken, and clear evidence provided of appropriateness to work with pupils as outlined previously.

External staff need to fully understand what they are expected to deliver and clear guidance on school policies, for example health and safety, behaviour management, should be given during any induction process. You may wish to observe the individual prior to fully recruiting their services. Many individuals may have a coaching background, but may not necessarily have in-depth knowledge of varying approaches to learning and teaching. You should ensure that appropriate references are obtained. Whitlam and Beaumont (2008) provides a comprehensive overview of criteria that need to be addressed when considering issues associated with safeguarding pupils.

Chapter summary

The aim of this chapter has been to look at how those involved in the teaching of physical education and the wider community can work together to provide effective learning experiences for primary school pupils. We have explored a range of issues associated with working with your secondary school, local facilities and external providers. Consideration must always be given to the safeguarding of pupils when using external providers or facilities. To consolidate your learning you should complete the following review questions.

1   What opportunities can you identify within your local area for interacting with the wider community?
2   What quality assurance criteria would you employ when working with community-based organisations?

Further reading

Green, K. (2005) 'Extra-curricular physical education in secondary schools in England and Wales: Reflections on the "state of play"' in K. Green and K. Hardman (eds), *Physical education: essential issues*. London: Sage. pp. 98–110.
While this book focuses on provision in secondary schools, it offers insight into developing and justifying extra-curricular provision as well as working with outside agencies.

Whitehead, M. and Pack, K. (2010) 'Working with others to achieve the aims of PE;' in S. Capel and M. Whitehead (eds), *Learning to teaching physical education in the secondary school,* 3rd ed. London: Routledge. pp. 52–64.
This chapter, again included in a secondary focused textbook, does provide further information concerning working with others in your own classroom as well as looking at engaging with the wider community.

CHAPTER 11

SUBJECT LEADERSHIP IN PHYSICAL EDUCATION

Chapter aims

- To develop an understanding of the role of the subject leader in physical education
- To identify the key skills and attributes associated with subject leadership
- To identify the key areas on which subject leaders should focus

The role of subject leader

Throughout this book we have looked at the concept of physical education and its practical delivery within the primary school. While it is expected that each class teacher will have responsibility for the lessons they plan and deliver, as the subject leader you will have the responsibility of co-ordinating the day-to-day aspects around the subject. Subject leaders 'provide professional leadership and management for a subject to secure high quality teaching, effective use of resources and improved standards of learning and achievement for all pupils' (TDA, 1998: 5).

While the role of subject leader has been embedded in the structure of a school for many years, recent changes in the structure and organisation of physical education, in particular the establishment of school sports partnerships, have resulted in many schools having primary link tutors. These are primary teachers who have received additional support and training to strengthen not only the primary physical education curriculum, but also the links that exist in physical education between primary and secondary schools. Their remit is focused on strategic planning; liaison within and between schools; the provision and development of extra-curricular activities; engagement with community organisations; engagement with external providers and raising pupil standards.

The role of the subject specialist in physical education is therefore focused on the management and co-ordination of schemes of work, pupil assessment, ordering and maintenance of equipment, and health and safety policy which includes risk assessment. They may also be asked to support staff development as well as co-ordinate staff who may come into the school to deliver aspects of physical education (for example outside coaches and adults other than teachers (AOTTs)). However, involvement extends beyond the core curriculum; they also co-ordinate extra-curricular provision as well as informing parents of what is taking place, for example sports day. Chapter 10 looked at how physical education can contribute to and be supported by the wider community. You may find it useful to combine the information in Chapters 10 and 11 as your roles and responsibilities increase.

It is clear that the responsibilities associated with leading a subject area are extensive. Integral to the success of the role is the leadership of the provision. Task 11.1 provides an opportunity for you to start thinking about what qualities are associated with good leaders.

 Task 11.1

1 From your own experiences, what do you think makes a good leader?
2 Looking at the characteristics you have identified, explain what these skills are and what they look like practically (for example, you might identify that a characteristic is associated with being organised, and this is reflected in always knowing what you are doing).
3 Finally look at the list in front of you and identify what skills you currently possess and what skills you would like to improve.
4 Produce an action plan to identify how you will go about developing these skills.

The next section looks at specific skills and attributes associated with leading a subject.

Skills and attributes associated with subject leadership

In Task 11.1 you will have started to identify a range of skills and attributes you would expect in a leader. The appointment of a subject leader for physical education should be based on an interest and level of competence in the subject. The appointee should demonstrate expertise in the delivery and organisation of the subject and be provided with support and training to achieve to the highest level. Such support may include subject-specific training as well as more generic training opportunities, for example nationally recognised leadership programmes.

Leadership and professional competence

It would seem to go without saying that a subject leader should already possess skills associated with leadership and professional competence. However, it is likely that many of you have been appointed to roles, and have learnt to develop similar skills on the job.

It is important that you have a clear focus, a common goal which you strive to achieve. When first thinking about taking a post in any subject area, you need to have a clear personal understanding of the aims of that subject and what you want to achieve (see Chapter 1). If you have confidence and a clear focus you are more likely to be able to lead staff in the direction you wish to take the subject. In many respects you need to be convincing so that people want to follow you. For many, teaching physical education is a challenge. You as the subject leader need to be able to support other members of staff, providing opportunities where necessary for them to grow in confidence in the delivery of the subject which will result in positive experiences not only for the teacher, but also for the pupils they teach.

Leading and managing staff can be one of the most difficult roles you undertake. While you might have a clear aim and focus in mind, not everyone will share it. At times you may have to reframe your expectations, for example if you want to introduce a different way of delivering lessons then you will need to plan how you are going to support staff in attaining the skills necessary to achieve this (you may find Chapter 3 helpful with this). You will need to work as part of a team, and it may be that part of your role is to delegate some responsibilities to others (although this will be very much dependent on the size of the school you work in). What is important is that you are clear about how changes you wish to make will impact positively on the learning of pupils.

Having identified your aims and focus for the subject, you will start to recognise priorities within physical education which may differ for different groups of pupils and staff and will require you to consider how the curriculum is structured and organised. As the 'leader' you will become a role model for both staff and pupils. While you have expectations of your team, they will also have expectations of you; don't be surprised if these differ! Some leaders find it useful to share their expectations with their team and produce some form of shared agreement of where you are going and how. This might be in the form of a rolling action plan which is updated at the end of each term, or a scheme of work based on feedback from class teachers and pupils.

However, leadership can be a lonely place and at times you may become despondent. What is important is that you share your successes, failures and frustrations with others. Throughout this book we have focused on developing your ability to reflect upon experiences and use them as learning opportunities. You might find it useful when first taking up a leadership role to identify someone who you can talk to, or keep some form of reflective journal and refer back to it. You might buddy up with another subject leader to share good practice and experiences, or work with colleagues from other schools who have a similar role to share experiences.

Problem solving and action planning

It is very easy to think that our main job in a leadership role is to solve problems. In fact I can remember one of my head teachers telling me that he didn't do problems, he wanted solutions. A statement such as this is somewhat cryptic but focusing on finding solutions to problems can be a more positivist approach to take. Having said that you will still have moments when you just don't see a solution.

The logical starting point when problem solving is to identify the problem or the issue that needs to be addressed. You need to be clear about the evidence you have available and how this can be interpreted. In the context of teaching the key focus must always be on the enhancement of pupil learning. A clear analysis of the issues should allow you to start to form an action plan to address them. At this point you may find that you need to refer some decisions to a more senior staff member or discuss your findings with the staff members involved. The case study at the end of the chapter provides you with an opportunity to follow through problem solving and action planning in a working example.

Communication skills

The ways in which we communicate have expanded over time. How we talk to people depends on the context in which this communication takes place, for example the way you talk in the staffroom may be very different to the way you talk in the classroom and the way you talk to parents. This also applies to the written word. We communicate to different groups of people, for example colleagues, governors, external organisations, parents, pupils via email, formal correspondence and pupil reports. As a leader, you have to think about who you are communicating with. It is important that you are clear about what you want to get across and the most appropriate way to do so, for example via email or a face-to-face conversation. Sometimes talking to the person, while potentially more difficult, will bring about a better resolution.

Self-management

As well as managing other people, you will also need to manage yourself. The pressures placed on us in our working life have increased over time. Time is an important commodity, and occasionally you might feel that we have none left for ourselves. Personal time management becomes important if we are to achieve what needs to be done in an efficient and effective manner, while preserving time for ourselves.

As the subject leader, you will need to identify your priorities and therefore action planning becomes an important aspect of your work. You will need to set long-term, medium-term and short-term goals. By having an understanding of what needs to be done and by when, you can more effectively manage your working day. By setting attainable targets for each day you can start to develop the capacity to detach yourself from work when at home. Many of you will have heard the term 'work–life balance'. What is important is that you are able to provide much needed down time for yourself or you many suffer 'burnout'.

So how can we self-manage? The key is to identify how we work best. For example, I know I work best first thing in the morning, and that depending on what I am doing I like to listen to music. However, I also know that I am easily distracted, therefore it might be better for me to complete certain tasks at home. Take some time to think about your own preferences for working and integrate these into your working day. You might find it useful to compile a diary of the tasks you complete during a week.

One frustration we all share is that we 'never seem to get anything done'. A solution is to identify the tasks that need to be completed (best done at the end of the previous day) including one key task that you want to achieve in that day, for example some marking, report writing, lesson planning. You should then aim to complete that task before anything else; by not checking emails and not answering phone calls for a set period of time you can become immersed in the job in hand. Once you have achieved that task you can go on to your next task. This gives us a sense of achievement even when the task is very small. If you are adopting such an approach you will need to build task time into your daily programme. This is a simple premise, but if you reflect on your week so far and compare what you wanted to achieve at the start of the week with what you have actually achieved you will see that building in 'task time' is not always as easy as it sounds.

We all have our own individual approaches to time management and self-management. What works for one will not work for another. It is therefore important that you identify a personal way of working which includes down time.

Time management is only one aspect of self-management. If you have achieved the position of subject leader, or are aspiring to become one, you should already have a focused approach to your personal career development. In order to have come into teaching you will have had to focus on the subjects you studied at school as well as the degree you achieved. Once you have qualified as a teacher, you do need to consider your continuing professional development. Most of you will be familiar with your career entry development profile which you completed at the end of your initial teacher education and will have used to set development targets throughout the first year of your teaching.

Throughout this book you have been encouraged to complete a portfolio identifying your own personal strengths and areas for further development. Taking responsibility for your own personal development is an important aspect of teaching. As subject leader you will also need to consider the developmental needs of those staff delivering the subject and provide structured opportunities for development to take place. It may be that you provide aspects of professional development yourself through training sessions, or that you engage external organisations to support this (see Chapter 10).

Similar to action planning, you should review your targets on a regular basis and this will form part of the dialogue you have with your line manager within your school as you assess your progress as part of any performance review process.

 Task 11.2

Reflecting on the list of development needs you identified in Task 11.1 and your emerging knowledge based on the previous section of this chapter, review your own action plan and identify three key areas of development you wish to explore over the coming year.

Strategic direction and development of the subject

As a subject leader, you will have aspirations around the development of your subject, however, you will need to work within the parameters set by the school. Each school will have a clear action plan or strategic plan around improving pupil learning and attainment. This will be shared regularly with you by the school management team, and your role as subject leader is to ensure that the plan is reflected in any planning you do. In essence you have to clearly define how you will achieve the school plan through your own subject plan.

Teaching and learning

We have identified that one of the key responsibilities of a subject leader is the management of effective teaching and learning of the subject area. You might find it useful to observe other staff teaching the subject as part of their own personal development. In doing so you will need to be clear about what the focus of your observations will be as well as how you will use your observations to support both the teacher observed and the development of the subject. You will also need to be clear about how you will deliver feedback drawn from your observations so that the process is seen as productive and not a threat.

It is likely that as a result of your observations you will be able to identify specific developmental opportunities. These should then be integrated into your rolling action plan.

Efficient and effective deployment of staff and resources

As well as managing your class, yourself and the curriculum, you are also likely to be managing a budget. While the amounts will not be large you will need to carefully consider your priorities and these should be included in any action planning you undertake. Maintenance is an important aspect of resource management. You should have clear guidelines about the use of the equipment with a specific focus on its storage.

You will have some form of equipment store. This should be kept tidy, with clearly defined storage areas. This will make the start of your lessons more efficient as you will find it easier to locate the equipment you need. Clear guidance on who is allowed in to the equipment store should be provided including whether pupils are allowed in, and who has responsibility for any keys. You might also include a log book where staff can record any damaged equipment or equipment losses (tennis balls in summer are the main ones here).

As the subject leader you will also have responsibility for aspects of health and safety within the physical education curriculum, and regular health and safety checks on equipment should be undertaken (see Chapter 5 for further details). Whitlam and Beaumont identify the following activities:

- Establishing systematic review procedures to encourage safe practice
- Carrying out risk assessments
- Inspecting apparatus and equipment on a regular basis
- Ensuring appropriate safeguarding provision is made
- Informing senior management of any safety concerns
- Leading on professional development relating to safe practice
- Communicating relevant safety information to all staff
- Maintaining an up-to-date staff safety handbook/policy
- Managing and overseeing the use of volunteers and coaches. (2008: 25)

Case study: Action planning

In your role as subject leader, it has been brought to your attention by the head teacher that attainment in physical education is lower that that of other curriculum subjects. The head teacher has requested that you look into ways this might be addressed.

The following key questions about current levels of attainment should be asked.

1   What are the current levels of attainment and how do these differ from other subject areas?

   a   When was the data collected?

      i   How old is the data being used?
      ii   Was it collected during or at the end of a term?
      iii   Was anything else happening when the data was collected?

   b   What data was collected?

      i   Was it related to performance of specific activities?
      ii   Was it related to overall attainment across the term/year?

   c   Is the data accurately reflecting attainment?

Having collected information regarding the situation you should be able to identify developments you might undertake.

   The following key questions about staff development and available resources should be asked.

1   Are staff confident in the assessment of performance in physical education?

   a   Do I need to provide any staff development opportunities?

      i   Should I involve outside agencies?
      ii   Should I look at cross-moderation of teacher's assessment?
      iii   Can I produce any support materials?

2   Are staff confident in the delivery of physical education lessons?

   a   Do I need to look at staff development opportunities?
      i   Are teachers using a range of teaching strategies within their lessons?
      ii   Are teachers differentiating to reflect the needs of all pupils?
      iii   Are teachers taking account of learning across the domains of learning?

3   Do we have enough equipment to support effective teaching?

   a   Do I need to look at requesting additional funding?
   b   Is funding being used effectively?
   c   Do I need to look again at how resources are being managed?

By drilling down to the problem and starting to look at potential solutions we can begin to add to our action plan.

Table 11.1   Action planning: raising attainment

Action	Success criteria
Develop resources and support materials for assessing performance in physical education	A range of assessment approaches demonstrated within lessons Pupils engaged in self and peer assessment against National Curriculum levels
Provide staff development opportunities around the delivery of physical education	Through lesson observations, staff demonstrate a range of teaching approaches Pupils report increased engagement in physical education lessons
Audit equipment management and storage	Improve standards of care and storage of equipment

In this case study your head teacher gave you a general observation of a problem. By asking questions you are starting to identify the source of the problem and in doing so beginning to identify possible solutions. For example, if you need to have more equipment so that pupils can practise their skills more frequently, do you need to negotiate an increase to your budget or undertake some fundraising activity? Do you need to provide some staff development on assessing pupils' performance and teaching strategies?

In completing this case study, you should have started to think about the integration of aspects of subject leadership into the development of action plans as well as looking at the range of factors which might impact on pupils' learning experiences.

 Chapter summary

The aim of this chapter has been to look at how you might develop in your role of subject leader for physical education in the primary school. The chapter has focused on the knowledge, skills and understanding associated with subject leadership, as well as looking at a range of strategies you could employ to move your subject further. What is important in the organisation of the physical education curriculum is that you continue to review and refresh your own knowledge, skills and understanding in order to ensure positive learning opportunities for your pupils and to support staff within the school. Regular engagement in professional development opportunities are of course to be encouraged. To review your learning you should reflect upon the following review questions.

1 What would you identify as the key characteristics of a subject leader?
2 What strategies would you employ to develop your competence as a subject leader in physical education?

Further reading

Dean, J. (2004) *Subject leadership in the primary school: a practical guide for curriculum coordinators*. London: DavidFulton Publishers.
This provides a comprehensive overview of the knowledge, skills and understanding necessary to lead subjects within the primary school.

Fleming, P. and Amesbury, A. (2001) *The art of middle management in primary schools: a guide to effective subject, year and team leadership*. London: Taylor and Francis.
This text provides more advice on not only supporting your development as a subject leader, but also other managerial opportunities within the primary school.

Raymond, C. (1998) *Coordinating physical education across the primary school (subject leaders' handbook)*. London: Routledge.
Focusing specifically on the co-ordination of physical education, this subject specific text book, while potentially dated, does provide additional support and guidance for the subject leader.

REFERENCES

Amos, S. and Postlethwaite, K. (1996) 'Reflective practice in initial teacher education: some successes and points for growth', *Journal of Teacher Development*, 5(3): 11–22.

Bailey, R. (2006) *Teaching physical education: a handbook for primary and secondary school teachers*. London: Routledge.

Bailey, R., Armour, K., Kirk, D., Jess, M., Pickup, I. and Sandford, R. (2006) *The educational benefits claimed for physical education and school sport: an academic review*. London: British Educational Research Association (BERA).

Bandura, A. (1989) 'Social cognitive theory', in R. Vasta (ed.), *Annals of child development, vol 6: Six theories of child development*. Greenwich, CT: JAI Press. pp. 1–60.

Bandura, A. (2001) 'Social cognitive theory: an agentic perspective', *Annual Review Psychology*, 52:1–26.

Bercow, J. (2008) *A review of services for children and young people (0–19) with speech, language and communication needs*. Nottingham: DCSF Publications. Available at www.education.gov.uk/publications/eOrderingDownload/Bercow_Interim_Report.pdf (accessed September 2011).

Bloom, B.S., Engelhart, M.D., Furst, E.J., Hill, W.H. and Krathwohl, D.R. (1956) *Taxonomy of educational objectives handbook 1: the cognitive domain*. New York: David McKay Co Inc.

Breckenridge, M.E. and Vincent, E.L. (1965) *Child development: physical and psychological growth through adolescence*. Philadelphia, London: W.B. Saunders Company.

Brunton, J.A. (2003) 'Changing hierarchies of power in physical education using sport education', *European Physical Education Review*, 9(3): 267–84.

Bunker, D.J. and Thorpe, R.D. (1982) 'A model of the teaching of games in Secondary Schools', *Bulletin of Physical Education*, 18(1): 5–8.

Capel, S., Zwozdiak-Myers, P. and Lawrence, J. (2003) 'A study of current practice in liaison between primary and secondary schools in physical education', *European Physical Education Review*, 9(2): 115–34.

Capel, S., Zwozdiak-Myers, P. and Lawrence, J. (2004) 'Information exchanged between primary and secondary schools about physical education to support the transition from Key Stage 2 to Key Stage 3', *Educational Research*, 46(3): 283–300.

Capel, S., Zwozdiak-Myers, P. and Lawrence, J. (2007) 'The transfer of pupils from primary to secondary school: A case study of a foundation subject – physical education', *Research in Education*, 77: 14–30.

Corbin, C.B. (2002) 'Physical activity for everyone: what every physical educator should know about promoting lifelong physical activity', *Journal of Teaching in Physical Education*, 21: 128–44.

Corbin, C.B. and Lindsey, R. (1997) *Concepts of physical fitness*. Madison, W.S: Brown and Benchmark Publishers.

Davison, J. and Leask, M. (2005) 'Schemes of work and lesson planning', in S.Capel, M. Leask and Turner, T. (eds), *Learning to teach in the secondary school: a companion to school experience*, 4th edn. London: Routledge. pp. 66–47.

Delignieres, D., Nourrit, D., Sioud, R., Lerpyer, P., Zattara, M. and Micaleff, J-P. (1998) 'Preferred coordination modes in the steps of learning complex gymnastics skill', *Human Movement Science*, 17: 221–41.

Department for Children, Families and Schools (2008) *The education of children and young people with behavioural, emotional and social difficulties as a special educational need*. London: DCFS.

Department for Education (1995) *Physical education in the National Curriculum*. London: HMSO.

Department for Education and Employment (1999) *Physical education: the National Curriculum for England*. London: HMSO.

Department of Education and Science (1991) *Physical education for ages 5–16*. London: HMSO.

Department of Education and Skills (2001) *Special educational needs: code of practice*. London: HMSO.

Department for Education and Skills (2002) *Learning through PE and sport*. London: HMSO.

Department of Education and Skills (2004) *Removing barriers to achievement: the government's strategy for SEN*. Nottingham: DfES Publications.

Department of Health (2004) *At least five a week – Evidence on the impact of physical activity and its relationship to health*. London: HMSO.

Erikson, E.H. (1995) *Childhood and society,* 2nd edn. London: Vintage.

Fleming, N.D. and Mills, C. (1992) 'Not another inventory, rather a catalyst for reflection', *To improve the academy,* 11: 137–55.

Fox, K. and Biddle, S. (1988) 'The child's perspective in physical education part 2: children's participation motives', *The British Journal of Physical Education,* 19(2): 79–82.

Gallahue, D.L. and Ozmun, J.C. (1995) *Understanding motor development: infants, children, adolescents, adults,* 3rd edn. Iowa: Brown and Benchmark Publishers.

Gardner, H. (1999) *Intelligence reframed: multiple intelligences for the 21st century*. New York: Basic Books.

Garhart Mooney, C. (2000) *Theories of childhood: an introduction to Dewey, Montessori, Erikson, Piaget and Vygotsky*. Minnesota: Redleaf Press.

Griffin, L.L. and Butler, J.I. (eds) (2005) *Teaching games for understanding: theory, research and practice*. Champaign, IL: Human Kinetics.

Haydn, T. (2005) 'Assessment for learning', in S. Capel, M. Leask and T. Turner (eds) *Learning to teach in the secondary school: a companion to school experience,* 4th edn. London: Routledge. pp. 301–24.

Haydn-Davies, D. (2005) 'How does the concept of physical literacy affect what is and might be the practice of Physical Education?' Available at: www.physical-literacy.org.uk (accessed September 2011).

Haywood, K.M. (1986) *Life span motor development*. Illinois: Human Kinetics.

Katz, L. (2003) 'The right of the child to develop and learn in quality environments', *International Journal of Early Childhood,* 3(1 and 2): 12–22.

Keenan, T. and Evans, S. (2009) *An introduction to child development,* 2nd edn. Thousand Oaks: Sage.

Kirk, D. (2005) 'Physical Education, youth sport and lifelong participation: the importance of early learning experiences', *European Physical Education Review,* 11(3): 1–16.

Kolb, D.A. (1984) *Experiential learning: experience as the source of learning and development*. New Jersey: Prentice-Hall.

Krathwohl, D.R., Bloom, B.S. and Masia, B.B. (1964) *Taxonomy of educational objectives; the classification of educational goals handbook II: the affective domain*. New York: Longman, Green.

Lawrence, D. (2009) *Enhancing self-esteem in the classroom*, 3rd edn. London: Sage.

Lawrence, J. (2006) *Negotiating change: the impact of school transfer on attainment, self-esteem, self-motivation and attitudes in physical education*. Unpublished PhD thesis. Brunel University.

McCaughtry, N., Sofo, S., Rovegno, I. and Curtner-Smith, M. (2004) 'Learning to teach sport education: misunderstandings, pedagogical difficulties, and resistance', *European Physical Education Review,* 10(2): 135–55.

Metzler, M.W. (2005) *Instructional models for physical education,* 2nd edn. Arizona: Holcomb Hathaway Publishers.

Morgan, P.J. and Hansen, V. (2008) 'The relationship between PE biographies and PE teaching practices of classroom teachers', *Sport, Education and Society*, 13(4): 373–91.

Mosston, M. and Ashworth, S. (1994) *Teaching physical education*, 4th edn. New York: Macmillan College Publishing Company.

Office for Standards in Education (2003) *Special educational needs in the mainstream*. LEA policy and support services (HMI 556). London: Office in Standards in Education.

Penney, D. (2003) 'Sport education and situated learning: problematizing the potential', *European Physical Education Review*, 9(3): 301–08.

Penney, D. and Waring, M. (2000) 'The absent agenda: pedagogy and physical education', *Journal of Sport Pedgagogy,* 6(1): 4–37.

Physical Education Association of the United Kingdom (PEAUK) (2003) *Observing Children Moving* (CD-ROM). Worcester: Tacklesport (Consultancy) Company.

Piaget, J. and Inhelder, B. (1969) *The psychology of the child.* London: Routledge Kegan Paul.

Qualifications and Curriculum Authority (QCA) (1999a) *The national curriculum for England: music.* London: DfEE and QCA.

Qualifications and Curriculum Development Agency (QCDA) (2010a) *The national curriculum: primary handbook*. Coventry: QCDA.

Qualifications and Curriculum Development Agency (QCDA) (2010b) *Introducing the new primary curriculum: guidance for primary schools.* Coventry: QCDA.

Rose, J. (2009) *Independent review of the primary curriculum: final report.* Nottingham: DCSF.

Schon, D.A. (1983) *The reflective practitioner: how professionals think in action*. London: Temple Smith.

Sheridan, M.K. (1991) 'Increasing self-esteem and competency in children', *International Journal of Early Childhood,* 23(1): 28–35.

Shilvock, K. and Pope, M. (2008) *Successful teaching placements in secondary schools*. Exeter: Learning Matters.

Shulman, L. (1987) 'Knowledge and teaching: foundations of the new reform', *Harvard Educational Review*, 15(2): 4–14.

Siedentop, D. (1994) *Sport education: quality PE through positive sport experiences.* Champaign, IL: Human Kinetics Publishers.

Simon, B. (1994) 'Why no pedagogy in England', in B. Moon and A. Shelton Mayes (eds), *Teaching and Learning in Secondary Schools*. Milton Keynes: Open University Press.

Simpson, E. (1971) 'Educational objectives in the psychomotor domain', in M.B. Kapfer (ed.), *Behavioural objectives in curriculum development*. Englewood Cliffs, NJ: Educational Technology Publications, Inc. pp. 60–67.

Smith, A. (1998) *Accelerated learning in practice: brain-based methods of accelerated motivation and achievement*. London: Network Continuum Education.

Smith, P.K., Cowie, H., and Blades, M. (1998) *Understanding children's development*, 3rd edn. Oxford, London: Blackwell Publishers.

Smith, A. and Thomas, N. (2005) 'Inclusion, Special Educational Needs, Disability and Physical Education', in K. Green, Hardman, K. (eds). *Physical education: essential issues*. London: Sage.

Social Policy Report (2010) *Autism spectrum disorders – diagnosis, prevalence, and services for children and children*. Society for Research in Child Development. Available at http://ea.nivsleadscape.org/docs/FINAL_PRODUCTS/LearningCarousel/ASDSocialPolicyReport.pdf (accessed September 2011).

Sugden, D.A. and Connell, R. A. (1979) 'Information processing in children's motor skills', *Physical Education Review*, 2(2): 123–140.

Teacher Development Agency (1998) *National standards for subject leaders*. London: TDA.

Teacher Development Agency (2009) *Including pupils with SEN and/or disabilities in primary physical education*. Manchester: TDA.

Vickerman, P. (2010) 'Planning for an inclusive approach to learning and teaching', in S. Capel and M. Whitehead (eds) *Learning to teach physical education in the secondary school,* 3rd edn. London: Routledge.

Whitehead, M. (2004) Physical Literacy: a debate. Paper presented at Pre-Olympic Congress, Thessaloniki, Greece, 2004.

Whitehead, M. (2005) Developing physical literacy. Paper presented at Primary Physical Education Conference, Roehampton, 2005.

Whitehead, M. (2009) 'The current working definitions of physical literacy'. Available at: www.physical-literacy.org.uk/definitions.php.

Whitlam, P. and Beaumont, G. (eds) (2008) *Safe practice in physical education and school sport*. Leeds: Coachwise Ltd.

Youth Sport Trust and Central YMCA (1998) *Fit for TOPs handbook.* Loughborough: YST.

Youth Sport Trust (2004) *TOP play and TOP sport student handbook: using TOP play and TOP sport in higher education institutions*. Loughborough: YST.

Youth Sport Trust (2005) *TOP play and TOP sport student handbook.* Loughborough: YST.

WEBSITES

British Gymnastics – www.british-gymnastics.org
Physical Education Resources – physicaleducationresources.com
Raising the Bar – www.creativedevelopment.co.uk/raising-the-bar
Rock-it-ball – www.rock-it-ball.com
Sports Coach UK – www.sportscoachuk.org
Wake Up Shake Up – www.wakeupshakeup.com
Youth Sport Trust – www.youthsportdirect.org.uk; www.youthsporttrust.org.uk

INDEX

TEACHING PRIMARY ENGLISH

Jackie Brien *University of Chester*

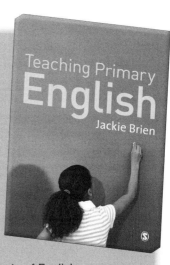

Literacy empowers learning across the whole curriculum and language is at the centre of all learning in primary education.

Aware of current curriculum developments and drawing from the latest research **Teaching Primary English** encourages teacher education students to develop a deeper understanding of the essential issues involved in teaching English in order to approach a career in the primary classroom with the confidence and knowledge required to succeed.

Taking a fresh approach to the main elements of teaching primary English, Jackie Brien strikes an engaging balance between the practical requirements of English teaching and encouraging informed reflection on key aspects of primary literacy.

Jackie Brien is Curriculum Leader for English, Communication, Language and Literacy at the University of Chester.

CONTENTS

What teachers of literacy know and do \ Speaking and listening \ Reading with and for understanding \ Teaching phonics for reading and writing \ Learning and teaching writing: the knowledge and processes of composing text \ Accuracy and presentation: the secretarial aspects of writing \ Inclusive learning and teaching of English \ Information and communication technologies in the teaching of English \ English and literacy beyond the classroom \ Planning to ensure progress in English \ Assessment and targeting in English

READERSHIP

Students studying primary English on primary initial teacher education courses including undergraduate, postgraduate and employment-based routes into teaching; also newly qualified teachers

December 2011 • 256 pages
Cloth (978-0-85702-156-4) • £60.00 / Paper (978-0-85702-157-1) • £19.99

ALSO FROM SAGE

CREATIVITY IN THE PRIMARY CLASSROOM

Juliet Desailly *Education Consultant*

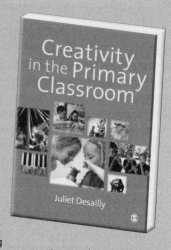

'This book deepens and broadens our understandings of creativity as applied to primary education. It provides a balance of practical frameworks and approaches with wise guidance. Many schools and individual teachers will find Juliet Desailly's work invaluable as they embrace the greater pedagogical and curricular freedoms promised by government.' - *Jonathan Barnes, Senior lecturer in Primary Education at Canterbury Christ Church University.*

Creativity is an integral element of any primary classroom. It has been never more important for teachers to involve children in their own learning and provide a curriculum that motivates and engages. Being creative involves generating new ideas, reflecting upon and evaluating different teaching approaches, and establishing an environment that supports creativity.

Creativity in the Primary Classroom explores how to develop as a creative teacher and how to foster creativity in your classes. Drawing from key literature and detailed real-life examples, Juliet Desailly puts into practice her extensive experience planning, advising and developing creative approaches to teaching and curriculum planning.

This book examines what creativity in a primary classroom can look like, and is supported throughout by practical activities for use across curriculum subjects and reflective tasks encouraging critical engagement with key conceptual issues.

This is essential reading for students on primary initial teacher education courses including undergraduate (BEd, BA with QTS), postgraduate (PGCE, SCITT), and employment-based routes into teaching, and also for practicing teachers wishing to enhance their own teaching.

CONTENTS

Section One: What is Creativity? \ The Key Elements of Creativity \ Creativity in Education: History and Theoretical Background \ PART TWO: A CREATIVE CHILD IN A CREATIVE CLASSROOM \ Building the Skills to Work Creatively \ Establishing the Ethos \ PART THREE: A CREATIVE TEACHER \ What Makes a Creative Teacher? \ Key Skills for the Creative Teacher \ PART FOUR: A CREATIVE CURRICULUM \ Planning for Creative Outcomes \ Medium Term Planning for Creative Outcomes \ Case Studies: Creativity in Practice

READERSHIP

This is essential reading for Students on primary initial teacher education courses, as well as practicing teachers wishing to enhance their own teaching

March 2012 • 176 pages
Cloth (978-0-85702-763-4) • £60.00 / Paper (978-0-85702-764-1) • £19.99

ALSO AVAILABLE FROM SAGE

PROFESSIONAL STUDIES IN PRIMARY EDUCATION

Edited by **Hilary Cooper** *University of Cumbria*

Developing an understanding of the professional aspects of teaching is an integral part of training to teach in primary education, and requires a broad and deep engagement with a wide number of practical and theoretical issues.

Professional Studies in Primary Education provides a wide-ranging overview of everything you will need to know to prepare you for your primary initial teacher education course, and your early career in the classroom.

Covering practical issues including behaviour management and classroom organisation, through to thought-provoking topics such as reflecting on your own teaching practice and developing critical thinking skills in the classroom, this textbook offers a modern and insightful exploration of the realities of teaching in primary education today. This approach is supported by:

- An awareness of current policy developments and statutory requirements
- Examining complex, multi-faceted issues in education
- Exploring alternative approaches to primary teaching practice
- Investigating ways to encourage personal and professional development as a teacher
- A companion website which includes extended essays adding further context to chapter content

This is essential reading for all students on primary initial teacher education courses including undergraduate (BEd, BA with QTS), postgraduate (PGCE, SCITT), and employment-based routes into teaching.

CONTENTS

PART ONE: INTRODUCTION TO PROFESSIONAL STUDIES \ **Susan Shaw** History of Education \ **Hilary Cooper** Philosophy of Education and Theories of Learning \ **Suzanne Lowe and Kim Harris** Planning, Monitoring, Assessment and Recording \ **Jan Ashbridge and Jo Josephidou** Classroom Organization and the Learning Environment \ **Jan Ashbridge and Joanne Josephidou** The Role of the Adults \ PART TWO: INCLUSIVE DIMENSIONS OF PROFESSIONAL STUDIES \ **Lin Savage and Anne Renwick** Reflective Practice in the Early Years: A Focus on Issues Related to Teaching Reception-Age Children \ **Verna Kilburn and Karen Mills** Inclusion and Special Educational Needs \ **Deborah Seward** Behaviour Management \ **Verna Kilburn and Karen Mills** Personal and Social Development \ **Donna Hurford and Christopher Rowley** Dialogical Enquiry and Participatory Approaches to Learning \ **Diane Warner and Sally Elton-Chalcroft** Race and Ethnicity: Teachers and Children \ PART THREE \ **Andrew Read** Reflective Practice \ **Diane Vaukins** Enquiry and Critical Thinking \ PART FOUR \ **Andrew Slater** Exploring Educational Issues \ **Nerina Diaz** Statutory Professional Responsibilities \ **Hilary Cooper** Moving into Newly Qualified Teacher Status

August 2011 • 272 pages
Cloth (978-0-85702-733-7) • £65.00 / Paper (978-0-85702-738-2) • £20.99 /
Electronic (978-1-4462-4989-5) • £20.99

ALSO AVAILABLE FROM SAGE